W9-CKL-330

The Prison of My Mind

The Prison of

My Mind

Barbara Field Benziger

WALKER AND COMPANY
New York

Fourth Printing

Published in the United States of America in 1969 by Walker and Company, a division of the Walker Publishing Company, Inc.

Published simultaneously in Canada by The Ryerson Press, Toronto.

Library of Congress Catalog Card Number: 69-14639

Printed in the United States of America

Dedicated to:
the late William A. Horwitz, M.D.,
the doctor who made me well,
and
Peter Benziger, my husband

For: My children

After all, no one can ever give the exact measure
of his needs, of his thoughts, of his sorrows.

Human language is like a cracked kettle on which
we beat out tunes for bears to dance to, when all
the time we are longing to move the stars to pity.

Gustave Flaubert, in *Madame Bovary*

Table of Contents

Introduction

For many centuries—long before there were professions called psychiatry and psychoanalysis—men and women have tried to write about their fears and sorrows in order to get distance on them and on themselves as suffering and struggling human beings, and of course in order that others will feel less alone and more hopeful. Certainly St. Augustine's *Confessions* ought to remind us that social and historical forces can account for only so much of man's behavior. In the fifth century Augustine could feel as lost and sad and troubled and anxious and guilty and bewildered as any twentieth-century citizen of industrial America. He could feel like nothing, absolutely nothing. He could consider suicide, even wish for it. He could feel hate in his heart, and love that somehow made matters worse rather than better.

And he could look into his mind and understand—and do so every bit as sensibly and shrewdly and correctly as any of us can, and by "us" I am including me and my colleagues, men trained in psychological analysis and introspection, but not always intelligent men or honorable men or kind men, as *The Prison of My Mind*, like other books before it, all too adequately demonstrates.

So, *The Prison of My Mind* shares a tradition that goes centuries back; but it also has more immediate roots. In 1907 an autobiographical book by Clifford Beers was published under the strong and direct title *A Mind That Found Itself.* A literate, intelligent man, Beers had gone "mad," with delusions and later a manic episode. Fortunately, he recovered—no thanks to the way he and others were treated in the asylums of that time. His book was in the muck-raking tradition: the cruelty and abuse directed at the insane were candidly set forth with painstaking care. And the book contained two letters to Beers from William James, in which America's greatest psychologist reminds Beers how important it is for psychologists and doctors to hear and understand what Beers experienced. Patients often do not realize how much they teach their doctors and how sheltered and sometimes unthinking a doctor can become.

Since *A Mind That Found Itself* appeared, psychiatry has made significant advances. No longer are thousands of patients openly and unashamedly and routinely chained and strapped and herded together like animals—and insulted and brutalized in a thousand less dramatic ways. Or so we think. The facts are not really available. True, in the 1940's a series of scandals and investigations caused many of the state hospitals to be reformed. Tightfisted legislatures voted more money, and psychiatrists began to be more available and more respected. That is a story in itself: the emergence of psychiatry as a respectable and indeed desirable medical specialty, capable of attracting to its ranks—not always, of course—able, intelligent, and kind young doctors. Still, for all the changes in psychiatric care, for all the understanding Freud's psychoanalytic insights have provided, for all the new tranquilizers and the "halfway houses" and the new clinics and the group therapy and occupational therapy, I still wonder whether thousands of troubled Americans really get a much better deal than Clifford Beers did in the very first years of this century.

Nor is it a matter of money, pure and simple as some of us tend to think. Barbara Benziger lets us know right off that she is not poor. Her experiences are those of a well-to-do woman who lives in a city all too well supplied with psychiatrists. She could afford the best, and she sought it. Yet, she found out something I'm not sure many people realize: not only do the rich suffer—hopefully, that *is* obvious—but they can pay a lot and get cheated, pay thousands of dollars and get no better care than a patient brought into any city or state hospital. The rich can be deceived and manipulated and lied to and cleverly, insistently, outrageously stripped of all dignity (and not a little cash). The rich can be made to feel as vulnerable, defenseless, and worthless as a pauper or a beggar—by the very people they pay so much to be of help. Barbara Benziger has not written her book to "expose" this or that institution; but quietly and unmaliciously she makes her point, that point: we are all potential victims of one sort or another.

When we are sick we tend to doubt even the best-intentioned people. When we get better we realize how unkind we have been. Still, generosity has its limits, and it is quite possible that many hurt and anxious people refrain from calling a spade a spade. When they are ill, they doubt their own reliability or "right" to protest this or that indignity. When they are recovered, they are so grateful to be among the psychologically living that old and bad memories are eagerly forgotten. It is a pity, because more people must have the confidence to judge not only themselves (most mental patients do far too thorough a job) but also their very keepers, helpers, doctors, whatever.

Recently I read Hannah Green's novel, *I Never Promised You a Rose Garden*, a beautifully wrought, touching, even haunting description of a schizophrenic woman's long, complicated, shaky effort to gain that elusive and hard-to-define thing we call "health." Barbara Benziger is no novelist, nor was she ever, at her most unhappy time, as confused and disorganized as Hannah Green was. But like her, she struggled hard for life, and in both cases the eventual outcome was not always clear. It would be foolish to hope that *The Prison of My Mind* will change things in American psychiatry, will make certain doctors stop and think a little more, and will help those patients or future patients who read it feel stronger–and better able to demand their rights. Yet, the attempts must be made–by Barbara Benziger and others too. We in America hear so very much from "experts," and prominent among them are psychiatrists. It is a good thing that now we have the words of one more so-called "lay person"—and how condescending *that* word can be. Barbara Benziger's words do not reveal anything new and revolutionary. They are not exquisitely polished and carefully weighed words. They are, though, the honest words of an intelligent and sensitive woman—who had enough courage, good sense, and social responsibility to sit down and write, share her life with us, so that we, like her, will not find everything shut off, even when that is how it feels. If I were upset, in despair, worried about whether there will be many days left, I would be grateful to people like Clifford Beers or Hannah Green or Barbara Benziger. They are not quite ready to let the matter rest with their own survival, their own victory. They have others in mind: the rest of us who are from time to time not so different from them.

We can only be grateful to them—and more hopeful because they and others like them continue to be among us, no matter how grim the world not only can seem but actually can be.

Robert Coles, M.D.

Foreword

Mental illness is not an orderly process. Although I have arrived at some degree of order today, much of this book remains as I wrote it under extreme duress. The form, therefore, is a bit irregular, but it has seemed to me to be the most honest way to present my experience.

The book consists of extracts from a journal I kept during and after my illness. When I was very ill, my notes were barely decipherable. I wrote, I now believe, in a desperate attempt to hang on to some shred of reality and sanity; also, perhaps, out of habit. For there had been many periods in my life when I had kept a diary, both as a child and as an adult.

I don't remember writing some of the notes. I had almost—but not quite—forgotten some of the incidents and feelings that they describe. After I was well again, my journal enabled me to go back and look at what I had written and to evaluate and analyze the whole experience.

At times I have made use of questions and answers between patient and doctor. I wrote down questions before my interviews with my doctor, wrote them, not only in order not to forget the extreme fears and tearing uncertainties that were pressing in on me, but also to shelve the feelings for the time being. It was as if someone else had shouldered, temporarily, emotions with which my sick mind could no longer cope. After an interview, I wrote down all the answers the doctor had given me, so that I could read and reread them during my worst moments, with the hope that they would bolster up my courage.

How extraordinary is the veneer of sanity and civilized behavior and thinking which continues to function most of the time, in spite of the deep disturbances and interior terrors that lie beneath it. Because of this veneer, it was possible for me to keep a testament, written almost as if I were under a spell.

My illness was diagnosed as a pathological depression, with suicidal tendencies and delusions. Intellectually, I was rational, but because of my depression, my state of mind took over to such an extent that I was misinterpreting and distorting reality. I was completely aware of every moment, and my faculty for recollection was more intensely developed than it had ever been, hauntingly so. During one period only did I lose my intellectual rationality and memory; that was during shock treatment.

All of us get depressed, and to some extent we all

entertain peculiar thoughts, fears, and fantasies. It is when they get out of proportion, become distorted and highly magnified, and push aside the rational conscious mind that one is mentally ill.

A depression such as mine induces such extreme feelings of hopelessness, self-deprecation, guilt, terror, endlessness, and despair that suicidal thoughts set in. I was aware at all times that I was not rational; therefore I sought help. Although I was in a state of indescribable anguish, I was luckier than a person who is unaware that he is not rational. My chances of getting well were hopeful. I believe I was fortunate in some ways to have had an "acute episode." Terrible as it was (and my doctor says that there is no anguish to equal that of a pathological depression), I think it was better to have lived through it, with the dire treatment it involved, than to have been semicrippled by emotions I could not possibly cope with for the rest of my life.

In the effort to understand my illness, I have come to know more about myself than I might have otherwise. With the help of a skilled doctor who enabled me to pick up the pieces of my life and put them together again in what I hope is an even better whole than heretofore, I have learned a bit about the problems of a mentally ill person. I believe it to be an endless process of learning, and sometimes a painful one.

I *had* to understand this eclipse of the mind. Why had it happened to me, and by what circuitous paths had I arrived at this condition of being? How far back in the past did it have its inception, and what kind of factors in my life had pushed me this far? What were the fears with which I finally had to come to terms in order to live and function?

In order to reach a point where I could view my illness from a better perspective, I had to relive many moments of my life, no matter how hurtful they had been to me.

After I was better, I looked back neither with the wish to blame others or, any longer, myself, nor with self-pity. Instead I had an overwhelming desire to comprehend, reevaluate, and reweigh my experience after all the searching of my mind and soul about my illness.

After I left the hospital, and as time went on, certain questions were put to me and statements made in front of me by intelligent and well-informed people that indicated a lack of comprehension about mental illness. What they referred to as a "nervous breakdown" is a term that in no way specifies any particular type of mental illness. I wanted to try to correct what I thought were prevalent misconceptions and mistaken attitudes about one type of illness–the one *I* had. More than anything else in the world, I wanted not only my children, family, and friends to understand it, but other people too.

I felt I must contribute my small measure toward a better understanding–not so much knowledge, but understanding. It is imperative for people to have a fuller capacity to feel for those who are mentally ill and understand how a person feels not only when he is ill but also when he is becoming ill and after he has been ill.

How could I get others to feel the feelings, the incredible and horrifying feelings with which you live during your seemingly interminable darkness? How could I lead them to understand that though you may be irrational, you are far from being "put away" and unaware of what is happening to you and around you? In your physical and mental prison, you are exceptionally aware of what is happening, more sensitive and more perceptive; and your power of receiving impressions is intensified to an agonizing degree. Each emotion, idea, thought, fear, like and dislike, love and hate, is magnified beyond recognition, and, along with your nerves, lies as if exposed on a surgical table, under a merciless light.

How could I convey, to some degree, some of the pain, the actual physical searing pain, which is impossible to describe wholly, that is ever present, as if your body were a reflection of the broken and tormented mind it contains; some of the terror of being completely and what seems irrevocably lost; the stark panic of finding every way "back" closed to you; the nightmare of delusions; the violent claustrophobia and agoraphobia which render you incapable of moving; the dreadful darkness of the dungeon of the mind; and most painful of all, the isolation, the complete isolation, the chasm between you and the rest of the world, across which there is no bridge, and your shouts for help cannot be heard? You live, or exist, with the agonizing feeling that you will be alone like this forever and ever. The people you love and have been close to may be there in reality, and yet they are not there. No one can help you, no one, and you no longer can help yourself. Yet if and when the people close to you stop trying to get through to you, if you feel they have stopped caring or loving you (and if this happens, you know and you remember), then whatever glimmer of hope you still retained of finding your way back to those you have loved and lost is shattered. Some wave of love, a little feeling of someone caring, does get through, and were it not for these efforts, you would be lost beyond recall.

It may help someone else to know that with my type of illness, given good care, though you may not believe it during your illness, there is an end to the dark tunnel in which you wander lost and alone for so long. There is an end, and an opening with a light to guide you back to the world you thought you had left forever. There will be detours, landslides, and lost ground, and you may despair, but there is an end and an out.

You are acutely, painfully, and unforgettably aware of the line, the fine line between the rational and the irrational, and the fact that you have crossed it. You will have a horror of crossing it again, which will become numb with time, if time is good to you. But in some dark little corner of your mind, the fear of recurrence, or "going back," will be there haunting you for a long, long time, possibly for the rest of your life.

It may help someone else to know how hard it is for every person who has had a mental illness to face the outside world again; but time spent in good mental health brings confidence, and though you may require years of after-care and help (for you must fight to stay well), you will stand alone someday, perhaps better than ever before. Certainly you are more acutely and poignantly aware of the priceless gift of life and freedom. Slowly, but appreciably, steadily, and surely, the bits and pieces and fragments fit together, and you find more of the "you" which was lost in the first place with the onset of your illness.

Life will never again be quite the same for anyone who has suffered through a mental illness, even if you are lucky enough to make a recovery. At the time of and right after the illness, the endless months seem totally irrelevant to the life that went before—monstrous—and above all, a tragic waste. And yet, perhaps, not such a waste after all. As an artist backs away from his easel in order to get a new and better perspective, it is possible to back off and begin to see the bad dream in a different light and from a different angle.

If I can help others to realize the depths to which the human spirit can sink, and the heights to which it can rise again; if I can lead them to the appreciation of the unrecognizable creature or thing I had at one time become, compared to the person I have become today, my story will have been worth the telling.

A friend of mine, a priest, said to me in the midst of my deepest despair, "Put every experience in life to good use, no matter how useless and painful it seems. You can't see how, at present, and you won't for a long time, but someday you will." I have not forgotten his words.

What follows, then, was written for myself at first, but finally for others—for those who must endure an illness, and for those who care about them.

1

The Onset

I think there can be no greater suffering than the state of mind I find myself in at present. I am sane enough to know that I am no longer sane. Somewhere, somehow, I am being dragged over a line, a line which never even existed for me until now. It's I, not someone else, but I, who am crossing that line, and I see no way to stop myself.

I have become, inexplicably, a wandering and completely bewildered stranger in the realm of my emotions. I can no longer find my way back to my familiar and known world where I *did* dwell *once* in some harmony with myself. Everyone is on the other side of an impenetrable glass. We can see each other, but we cannot reach each other, and I am stretching out my hand in vain. I am alone and abandoned in the dark, and I am terrified, beyond any understanding, and the *not understanding* leaves me in a state of paralyzing panic.

I can't move in any direction.

I am becoming more and more rigid physically. I am afraid that if I turn my head, even a little, I will *see* my horrible terrors and they will overwhelm me. I think I'm being followed, inexorably followed—I am running through endless, twisting, pitch-dark tunnels, and I can't find my way out. There is no light at the end of any turn I take. I can't turn back. I am being backed into the darkest and last corner of all. (Oh, yes, I know it's not rational, but I can't stop thinking these monstrous thoughts.)

I long to escape from these feelings that I can neither understand nor bear. Where is there a place for me, where can I go, where can I turn, save deeper and deeper into the labyrinth of my poor sick mind?

My mind is dying and I want to die with it.

The pain is too much to bear.

Even my body hurts.

My terrors are crushing me, smothering me. I can't breathe—I can't communicate my fears to anyone with any hope that they will be understood. I am locking myself up in a prison of my own making, a horrible, painful prison, to which I have no key.

There is only one escape, and that is death. I plan each day and night how to take my life. It is hard to believe that I, who loved life so much, am planning to kill myself—find myself longing for death. I am obsessed with one desire—to blot out a mind that can harbor and play with such thoughts.

Someone must help me—save me from myself, for what will become of me?

I don't really want to die.

The Fissure

How long had this state of mind been in the making, and what had triggered it? I remember vividly an episode that made me begin to doubt my sanity.

In July my husband and I took our four children to a ranch in Wyoming. I was thrashing down my favorite stream in my waders, slipping and sliding on the wet rocks, with my trout rod in one hand, and two trout with a stick threaded through their gills in the other, humming away happily. I was thinking, "How I love this country, and how I love fishing. They give me such a sense of peace."

The wind was blowing off the mountains. On one mountaintop there was a big patch of snow. I could smell the pine trees and could almost feel the snow. I felt an extraordinarily acute sense of well-being and delight in my surroundings—one of those rare moments in your life when everything seems right, and time appears to stop for an instant, so that you become aware of an infinitely precious moment. In fact, it was all so beautiful and perfect, I wanted to cry, because these moments come so seldom, and they are so quickly gone.

I sat down on a log to change my fly to a brighter one, because the sun was beginning to go down. I was feeling quite elated. I had found a deep, dark-green, very fishy-looking pool, where I was sure a big, fat, record-breaking trout would be lurking. I took time out to munch on a peanut-butter sandwich and to smoke a cigarette.

I shut my eyes to listen to the rush of the stream over its rocky bed and the wind from the mountains rustling through the leaves of the aspen trees behind me. I thought, "How much are we a part of what we see and feel, and *how* we see it and feel it." I wanted this moment to go on forever.

When I opened my eyes to get on with the fly-tying job, suddenly I felt something had gone wrong. I had a terrible sense of dread, and I was overwhelmed by panic—all the more inexplicable because of my feelings and thoughts just seconds before. I could not move. I hurt all over—in my heart, my body, and my head too. I said to myself, "What's wrong, you idiot? Get up and take a look around." But when I did, I thought I saw bears all around me, converging on my bend of the stream, closing in on me (we had seen a bear at a distance, out riding, a few days earlier). Why were they after me? Did they want my fish? I looked around frantically for a way to escape, and in my panic I forgot where I had tied my horse. The terror became unbearable. I flung my fish to the ground and plunged into the stream and tried desperately to wade against the current, hoping the bears could not swim. The stream was near freezing and the current was strong. It was like a nightmare in which you try to run and cannot. My legs behaved as if they were made of putty. It was like being caught in quicksand.

Where *was* my horse?

Finally I struggled up the steep bank of the stream, running over rocks and fallen trees. I could not find the patch of aspens where I had left my horse. My throat was so dry I felt I was choking. My heart was beating as if it were going to burst, and my chest felt as if it would no longer contain it. It was like holding a wounded wild bird in your hand; all you can feel is its heart, beating, beating, against the walls of its little body. Even in my panic, I thought of the little wounded bird my children had adopted a week or so ago. It had died, and they had buried it outside of our cabin and put a tiny wooden cross over the spot, which someone had deliberately kicked down. They had cried, and I had cried inside too. Now the tears were streaming down my face. I felt rain, I heard thunder, I saw lightning. The wind had increased to hurricane proportions; the rain had turned to sleet. Why was it suddenly so dark? I ran frantically through a clump of trees, catching my rod and line on the branches. I dropped the rod, groped through the trees—and ran right into my horse. He was munching peacefully on a branch, just where I had left him.

What had happened to me? I looked upward. The sky was a cloudless blue; there was an afterglow lingering across the valley, from the sun setting behind the highest mountains. High up, an osprey glided. I could see his nest on top of a tall, dead tree, far away. There was no rain. No wind. No thunder. No lightning.

And there were no bears.

Trembling with cold from my immersion in the stream, I put my face against my horse's side and wept.

Later, I went to retrieve my rod and rode back to the ranch through the dusk—such a peaceful time of day—badly shaken. My terror had passed but was replaced with a sickening sense of dread, of something totally unknown, unimaginable, unthinkable, and above all, *not to be shared with anyone*.

Just moments ago I had been so joyous in my aloneness; now I was isolated in a different kind of aloneless, and I was frightened beyond description. This was a kind of lonely aloneness to be feared. I felt I might not be able to get out of it, ever. Where might it lead me? I would have to cling to people now, to keep away any more of this type of thing. I who loved so much to be alone could no longer trust myself to be alone.

The Crack Widens

I think I slipped down the next step five months later, in December, when my husband and I went to Florida with the children. I had developed a kidney infection on the train, so we stopped at Jacksonville, where I was left in a hospital, while the children and my husband went on to our original destination.

I felt completely and unreasonably abandoned. The drug that I was given by the doctors was not agreeing with me, and I was panicky. I was becoming obsessed with drug reactions. I had had serious ones in the past, where my throat swelled up and I couldn't breathe. I was afraid that a new doctor would pooh-pooh my past allergic reactions, and was frightened to try the drug he had ordered for me, especially since he would not tell me what it was. Half the time I took the pills because I hurt so, and half the time I pretended I had taken them and hid them in the side of my mouth, swallowed water, and disposed of them later.

As soon as I could stand up, I took a plane, a two-seater, to fly me to where the children were. In the plane I was overcome by a violent feeling of claustrophobia. I had never had this feeling before in the air. Hitherto I had neither liked nor disliked flying. I was only a little afraid of it at times when the weather was bad. This time I had to control myself not to scream and break the windows and tell the pilot to come down—anywhere. I thought, "Suppose the pilot dies—I will fly forever and forever into the sun like a moth into the flame of a candle." I felt the sun was sucking me up. I had the feeling, one which would become only too familiar, alas, that I was going to run *amok*. I don't know quite what I meant by that term, or what I would do if I *did* run *amok*, but the thought and the word paralyzed me with panic.

Later, coming back from Florida on the train to New York, I was lying on my bed in my compartment with a very lovable stray cat we had adopted, or rather that had adopted us. Suddenly he looked much too big, and I flung him off the bed in terror. I burst into tears, because I really loved him, and I had hurt him. I ran to the club car to join the children, trying to feel normal.

Back in New York in April I went to seek psychiatric help, because I knew I was losing my grip on myself, and my marriage was in part responsible. My only salvation was in this doctor on whom I focused all my hopes. He *had* to make me better.

One evening in the spring, one of my children and I were walking up Madison Avenue back to our apartment in New York, after a happy afternoon of shopping. Suddenly we were caught in a pelting downpour of rain. At first we both got the giggles; we didn't have raincoats, rainhats, or umbrellas.

My daughter did the logical and sensible thing and

jumped into the first bus that came along. The bus was jammed. I had one foot on the step of the bus and was about to climb on, when all at once I could not get on that bus. I was afraid of where it might be going, and I could not stand the thought of being packed in and trapped with a lot of people. I jumped off the step, pushing people behind me aside, ran through the streets in the soaking rain, and arrived dripping and on the verge of hysteria at the apartment. What could I tell my child that would make sense? She knew something was wrong, and she was old enough to be concerned, but I didn't know what was wrong myself.

I spent all of that night in a shivering panic. I was afraid to look at the windows. I was terrified that I was going to be compelled to jump out of one. About four in the morning, I moved into the bathroom, which had no window, lay on a bath mat, and went to sleep.

Soon I could no longer go to theaters or movies. If I went, I had to run out of them. Riding the elevator in the apartment house or in any store was a torture. Never did I discuss weather so assiduously with the elevator men, to take my mind off my terror. Self-service elevators were out of the question. I could no longer visit people who lived in buildings that had no elevator men in the elevators, unless they were kind enough to come and fetch me or unless I could walk up and down the stairs. I could no longer use the tunnel to get to Long Island from New York City.

Gradually I arrived at the point where I could not use subways, buses, trains, planes, boats, and finally taxis and my own car, unless I could stop at any moment, anywhere, and get out. I was ashamed to be driven, because I thought the driver would think I was crazy (and he would be right) if I had to jump out of the car frequently.

In the early summer we moved from our apartment to a new house in the country. I remember drifting around the apartment in a daze of drugs (I was on all kinds of tranquilizers by this time), trying desperately to tag things for the house, things for storage, things to be sold with the apartment. The effort to do this coherently was such that I could hardly breathe. My lungs, my stomach, and my legs had a funny "all-gone" feeling. The objects I tagged seemed to be floating in a spaceless kind of world. I wanted to play the piano, usually a source of much pleasure to me, but I could not go near it, no matter how hard I tried.

I had a craving, an overpowering compulsion, to get everything settled and unpacked all at once in this new house, as if there were no time left, as if *external* order in the house might produce *internal* order inside me. Consequently I worked way beyond the limits of my strength, late into the nights.

The Rope Snaps

After we had been settled and I was beginning to love the new house, I was in the attic one evening, pushing suitcases and boxes around, trying to stow away things like Christmas ornaments, when I felt a crack in my head, as if it had split down the middle—a complete division. I had a mental picture of one of Picasso's two-headed women. I felt like two people. I sat down on a suitcase and held my breath. Had I had a stroke? I wasn't paralyzed, at least not actually—only by fear. I felt no numbness anywhere, and I remember saying something to see if I could speak properly. Something had snapped in my head like a too tightly drawn string on a guitar.

It was the strangest sensation I had ever had. There had been no warning that it was going to happen. One moment I was fine, working, thinking logically; the next moment, with no apparent shifting of gears, I was an entirely different person—two people, in fact.

I did not know what had happened to me or how I had got to where I was. At that moment, the anguish that flooded through me cannot be described. Everything was totally unfamiliar—a barren, desolate wasteland. I realized remotely that a complete, devastating crackup was in store for me.

That night the noise of water running in and out of a fountain outside my window in the rose garden, a sound I generally loved because it sounded a little like a stream, became unbearable. I slammed all the windows shut and put my head under the pillows.

A woodpecker had been visiting us every morning and had been hammering on a piece of metal with which we had covered the tops of our chimneys to keep out squirrels. One morning he made such a deafening noise, I felt the whole house tremble. The noise echoed and reechoed through the rooms, thundering in every corner as if the plumbing had gone berserk all over the house, and all the pipes had become human and were screaming to be let out of the walls that enclosed them. I lay awake every morning waiting for the woodpecker, dreading his coming, and dreading his not coming.

Now the bureau that I had had since I was a child

was beginning to threaten me. It was trying to crush me. It was developing a sort of face, and it was moving.

I did not dare go to the village. I was sure I looked queer and that people were whispering about me. I looked in the mirror. I did not look like the *me* I once knew, but I had not developed a hump or deformity that showed.

I was trapped in the house. I could not phone anyone; they'd know I was queer. I could not answer the phone either, because I could not talk to anyone sane. I thought, "No one likes me, no one comes near me, no one cares. I do not want them near me anyway—there's something terrible I can't tell them. They mustn't come to call; I will run and hide if they do; yet never have I needed people more and never have I been less able to see them."

If I went out, I thought, "I am being followed." I tried to hoe the weeds in the garden, but I couldn't finish the job. I hate to leave a job undone or unfinished. But "they" were watching me and following me, and "they" frightened me to such an extent that I couldn't even do that simple task. I thought that I must have done something awful to be followed that way.

I wanted to go in the swimming pool. It was too cold and deep. Everything was cold, yet everyone kept saying it was the hottest summer in years. I felt cold; I felt the *weight* of it. It pressed in on me, on my heart, on my stomach, on my body, and on my mind.

I tried to leave the house to seek comfort in my children, to reassure them that I could still do things with them. They drove me to the club one day, and we tried to play tennis. I was so weak and uncoordinated—I couldn't follow the ball or keep my mind on it. I was unseeing, unknowing, and unhearing. I had to ask my son to take me home. I was terrified. Of what? If I only knew.

Poor children, did they know what was happening to their mother—what she was thinking? If they did, how horrified they would be, and frightened. I did not think the show was fooling them, but I hoped it was. I wanted to hug them, clutch them to me, to say, "Never let me go." I wanted to say, "I am slipping so far away from you, and I need you more even than you ever needed me," but there was pride and the wish not to frighten them. I must use iron control—what's left. I must hide in my room, because the control is getting less.

I tried taking the children to Coney Island. I wanted so much to stay part of their lives, and share things, and laugh with them as we had so often done. I looked in the funny, distorted mirrors. We all laughed and shrieked, but inside something told me, "You really look like this. Your mind is like this. It must show outside as well as inside." I had feared the roller coaster. I thought the children were disappointed in me. I closed my eyes and blocked my ears while going endlessly through the dark tunnel of love, because I felt trapped in the crowd and I wanted to get out and run ahead of the train on the track. The sudden noises and shrieks hurt my head. The crazy house, with lopsided rooms—were they lopsided or was I? I was pale and shaken. The children fed me a pizza pie; they were worried and suggested we go home.

How touching are children who grow up to worry

and care and try to be protective, but I did not want them to have these feelings about me. My children must grow straight and free of this kind of "thing." They did not know quite what was wrong, and I could not put it into words—not words they would understand; I did not understand it myself.

I must have been very distraught. The children would say, "Where have you been? You are not listening."

"I don't know," I would answer.

I felt I'm there and I'm not there, and I know they feel it, and I know they are there, and yet they are not there, to me. I wanted to ask them, "Who am I? Please tell me. Do you belong to *me*, or *I* to you?" But they were too young to guide me back to my previously known world. If they, with their love, could not, who could?

I tried going to a party, and I think I was the only one to stay sober (drinks and drugs don't mix), and my stomach ulcer, which had been bothering me for almost a year, was raising hell. Liquor was no escape for me. But I knew I was the only one there off balance. I am very nearsighted. If I don't put my glasses on, everything is blurred; yet, when I put them on, they made everything too big. I tried to answer questions through a dense fog. I doubt if my answers made much sense, but then I doubt if the questions did either. I don't think anyone was making enough sense to know that I wasn't making any. I looked at people and thought, "Suppose I come right out and shout, 'You know, I'm terrified that I am being followed, and that's why I keep looking behind me! Do you see anything too? And do you know that I am not sane?' " Oh, what was the use, I couldn't say such a thing and I could not make flippant conversation! I was being backed more and more into a corner, so I fled.

All I knew was that I was more and more removed from my surroundings. Everyone looked different and strange—even the people closest to me.

I was outside of myself, watching me all the time. This had happened occasionally in the past—I would be looking at myself doing something—but now I could not merge the two anymore. I wanted to stop looking at me from the outside, to get back into the inside of me. A small part of my brain remained sane enough to look at the insane part with horror.

My God, if I could only sleep. Insomnia had become an obsession. I lived in a haze of tranquilizers, sleeping pills, and other medicines to keep me sane, I suppose, but there was no blessed oblivion and no sleep. There was only endless wakefulness with no escape. The more I tried to sleep, the less I slept. "Eternal sleep would be the only peace for me now," I thought, "where there would be no room for these horrors that keep running through my head. Oh, God, anything to end these endless minutes like hours. Time stands still—it has stopped forever. Has a second gone by?"

When you are well, there is never enough time for the things you love and care about and want to do and accomplish. Now I started at daybreak to dread time, so I began to make plans to protect myself against the next night and that awful brain that would not be turned off. If I slept, a drugged sleep, I had nightmares that dragged me into horrible places where I did not want to go.

Either they had been buried all these years or I did not know they existed. And the nightmares did not stop when I woke up; they continued. I no longer knew what was real or what was a dream. When I awakened, I had to identify each object in my room in order to identify myself.

"Disorder" of the mind is a good word. I, such an orderly person, couldn't make any order out of the chaos.

The intellectual and the emotional were so intertwined that I could not separate them—or else they were so separated that I couldn't get them to meet; I did not know which. Everything emotional, I could put on an intellectual level, and say to myself rationally, "This is not rational." I could take an emotion like panic and put it on an intellectual and thinking level. "What is this panic?" I could ask myself quite rationally about my irrational thought that I was being followed, and answer, "No one is following you, so why panic?" But the intellect seemed to have lost touch with the emotions—some line was down, as in a storm.

One of my strangest and most devastating situations was my inability to pick up a newspaper, book, or magazine or even to look at television without identifying myself with every bad thing in it. I seemed to have taken on the guilt of the whole world.

I picked up my children's edition of Beatrix Potter's *Peter Rabbit* because the pictures comforted me, but I wept at the end because I had never given my children camomile tea—even a rabbit had a better mother than I had been. Had I done something good once?

How strange that terror, overwhelming terror, should be so inarticulate! I wished I could just scream and beat my head against the wall. Instead I paced and paced around the house, or I was frozen, immobile, paralyzed, afraid even to turn my head for fear of shaking loose my brain from its moorings—its once sure, safe, and familiar moorings.

"Where am I and what am I? I have lost the bit of me that I once was. I'm a complete nonfunctioning nonentity, with no identity that I can hang on to—lost—lost—lost. There is no me, no self—I don't exist; yet I must exist, to suffer so."

It would never end, would it? Not if I didn't end it. A mind like mine was now could never get well. The children were the only brake that stopped me from killing myself.

Why had I turned so completely against myself—not against anyone else, not against the world, but just against myself? How could people think that people who were not rational did not feel? If I were the kind of disturbed person who thought she was Queen Victoria all her life, and remained safe and happy in this delusion, and never came out of it, I believed I would find life more bearable. Total madness would be a release.

It was getting harder and harder to drag myself three times a week to the doctor's office alone. My heart beat so I could not breathe when I started to go there, and before I dared go in the door, I had to walk around the block at least once. Was I afraid I could not tell the doctor those terrible thoughts of mine, or was I afraid of what he would say when I did tell him? Did it bother me that there would not be time in an hour to tell him everything? Was I afraid that I would withhold some things because they were so terrible? No, this I would never do. After all, I had asked him to help me, and in order to help me, he must know me as I was.

When I went into his waiting room, I resented all the other people who were there taking his time. Some of his patients looked strange, and all appeared to be shrouded in a veil of mist. In fact, I felt as if we were all at the bottom of an aquarium. "Good God, do I look as distraught as some of the other patients?" I asked myself.

I hid behind a magazine. I knew the doctor gave shock treatments there, and this was in part what caused my panic. I knew that was why some patients were accompanied by a relative or a friend. I did not dare ask the doctor if he thought I needed shock treatment.

After seeing the doctor, I talked to his nurse. Even though she was too busy to talk, she did for a while each time. I did this just so I could stay a bit longer in the safety of the office; although it terrified me to come, it terrified me more to leave—for where would I go?

I would leave the office and wander through the streets, uncaring if I was run over—aware that once or twice taxi drivers had yelled at me. I would have to hang on somehow until the next appointment with the doctor.

The last interview went something like this:

Me: "I don't exist anymore; there is no me."

Doctor: "But I see you sitting on the other side of the desk from me. Aren't you?"

Me: "Yes, but I've lost my mind, so I am not really here."

Doctor: "You came here alone, didn't you?"

My eyes focused on the paper cutter on his desk. I tried to concentrate on his voice. "Please, voice, never stop, help me find my mind. Please help me fight for my life, please help me find myself."

Me: "You must do something. Do you know what I did since I last saw you? I tried to get my shotgun out of our gun cabinet. We always keep our shotguns locked up, and I could not get at the guns. I was going to kill myself. Where do you think I must go? You must have me put away. Why, why am I thinking of doing these dreadful things? I am stark raving mad. You must stop me; you've got to." I could hear myself shrieking.

Doctor: "Now, look, you are not going to take your own life, and you are not raving mad."

Me: "I'm crazy, I'm thinking crazy things. You know it's crazy to want to kill yourself, and the fact I want to do it must mean I am crazy."

Doctor: "But you have not killed yourself. You say you think of nothing else—yet you come to me and you want me to stop you."

Me: "I haven't done it, because I know I am insane. This isn't me, it's someone else. Oh, God, to think I tried to do what I told you."

Doctor: "You will get over this."

Me: "No, I will never get over it. I can't rest, I can't stay still, not with this plan in my head. My mind won't stop ticking. It begins at dawn, it goes all through the night, begins again at dawn; it never stops, I go upstairs and downstairs, I can't go out of the house. Or I just sit and can't move. I can't eat. It is as if I had dropped a stone in the water, and the circles went on growing and growing and growing, and they never stop, and they hurt my head."

Doctor: "Never mind now. . . . "

Me: "But I do mind—there's so much—I can't stand it. There's a voice in me that says, 'Kill yourself,' and one that says, 'Don't kill yourself.' I hate this fog of drugs I'm in—I tell you, my head is divided in two. Do the two sides of my face look different? No, don't look at me, no one should look at me."

Doctor: "You look the same as always to me, only more miserable. Why do you think you've lost your mind?"

Me: "There is no me anymore, so how can I tell you about losing my mind? It doesn't matter about killing myself—my mind is dead already."

Doctor: "You are here, aren't you?"

Me: "Yes."

Doctor: "If you are here, then your mind must be here too."

Me: "Oh, what's the use of anything? Nothing is the same—it never will be again. I can't carry around these thoughts and terrors anymore. It all gets more and more unbearable. I will do something awful to myself."

Doctor: "Now, I am right here, and nothing is going to happen to you. You will not kill yourself, because I will not let you. I will help you, and we will get you well, you and I."

Me: "What is wrong with me?"

Doctor: "You are temporarily emotionally very disturbed. This does not mean that you will not get well."

Me: "You've got to protect me—from me."

Doctor: "I am going to put you in a hospital."

Me: "What kind of hospital? Locked?"

Doctor: "Let's say it's a hospital geared to your needs at present."

Me: "Oh, God . . . what horrible, ominous words."

2

The "Bad" Hospital

Last night I was bundled into a car, dimly aware of beloved but now unfamiliar children, dogs, house, all disappearing in a blur, and driven by my husband to the hospital "geared to my present needs."

I entered a room where there were several doctors who introduced themselves. I signed some paper in a daze, but nothing anyone said made any sense to me. I was too frightened and drugged. I didn't even have enough sense to try to read the paper I signed.

I was taken to my room. I noticed that the windows were barred, and my heart sank even further.

A nurse helped me unpack, and my husband left. There I was, alone and abandoned.

I was relieved of cigarettes, matches, cosmetics, manicure set, razor and razor blades, pins, scissors, knitting needles, needlework needles, and money. Why this last indignity? I hadn't planned to go on a wild spending orgy.

I asked, "What if I want to make a phone call?" I was informed that phone calls were not permitted at any time. I was stupefied by the finality of this rule. "Can't I even call home?" "There are no exceptions to the rule" was the answer.

I was told that I could write letters, but to leave them unsealed on the hall desk, because the mail was censored. "My God," I thought, "they must have something to hide."

A rather cross-looking old woman came into my room and locked my clothes closet, my bureau, and my bathroom. "But I have to use the bathroom during the night," I protested.

"That's your problem," she said with a very strong Scotch burr.

"It's going to be yours too, believe me. Can't I have a wee potty to get me through the night?" I asked, thinking wistfully of my old Scotch nanny.

"I'm not in the least sure I can find one. We haven't had a baby in here before."

"You bitch," I thought.

"You're being taken off all drugs, ye know," she went on relentlessly, "so you may not sleep overly well."

"That," I thought, "is the understatement of the year. I should have been sent to that place in Kentucky. I'll be crawling up the walls. There, at least, they wean you off drugs by degrees."

One of my worst obsessions now is my inability to sleep. I would like it to be an eternal, dreamless sleep. On the other hand, I dread sleep because my nightmares are so ghastly. They have to do with benches covered and jammed with disheveled, deformed, idiotic-looking people, all reaching for a high window. People in white are running around with huge needles and threatening everyone. Inside this room with the benches there are small children, crying from closed-in cots, and no one hears them. I am trying to climb a staircase to the window, and yet there is no staircase. Once I succeeded in getting out of the window, and I hid under some stairs outside. There were dreadful snakes and spiders and rats crawling all over everything. I keep wanting to get out of that window in my dream, and yet I don't want to, because the one time I was outside, the world was a desolate waste, with only the snakes and the spiders and the rats overrunning it.

Since I was unable and unwilling to sleep, I stood in the middle of my room and considered what to do. I examined the window and poked a hole through the screen with a bobby pin I had taken out of my hair; this act made me feel better.

My God, if my mail is censored, I can't pour my heart out to anyone, including my lawyer. I'll have to write lies, and say the place is great, that I am fine, I hope you are well, etc., like a six-year-old writing home.

I heard them lock the door to my room. I ran and pounded on it and screamed, "Why do you lock my door?"

Bonnie Scotland came back and said, "For a few days we are going to."

"But you can't," I yelled. "I have terrible claustrophobia. I won't leave my room. Please don't lock it."

"Orders are orders."

"Whose orders?" I asked.

No answer, and the door remained locked. I thought, "Why? My room is right near a desk where there is an attendant; the great, thick wooden front door of the place is locked and bolted." I saw that much when I first came in the place. A battering ram wouldn't break it down. This is the crowning blow. I am trapped like an animal–suppose there were a fire? I couldn't stay in here and pound on the door forever, or beat my head against the wall. I'm going to get out of this place; so help me God, I'll break out somehow. I'll use what remains of my brain to plan how to do it.

I lay down on my bed and repeated over and over, "Please don't cage me in this way. I will become more and more insane." What is this prisoner, criminal attitude? I don't get it–I haven't done anything wrong. I'm just sick and need help. I asked for protection, but not Alcatraz, for God's sake. Why didn't they mention all these delightful rules and prohibitions while my husband was still here, and before I signed anything?

My husband could not visit for a few weeks, until I "adjusted." Well, I was not going to adjust, because I'd never get well in the place, never.

God, it was rough being hauled off drugs just "bing" like that. I suppose they wanted to see how bad I'd get, damn them.

I lay rigid on my bed, and I was homesick –homesick like a child who has never left home for a night.

I wished that eyes that once looked out would stop looking in all the time. All right, I'll study every detail of this wretched room.

The door opened. "Why isn't your light out yet?"

"I can't sleep."

"Well, you can't sleep with your light on, so put it off."

I got up off the bed, went over to the bureau, and tried to see myself in the mirror by the light of a full moon. Was the mirror queer, or was I? I looked like a complete stranger. I seemed more like a distorted shadow of myself than the real me. Even by moonlight I could see that I was thin and haggard. I hadn't eaten much during the past few months. A phrase my nanny used to say came back to me: "Eat one spoonful for me, dear, if not for you." Maybe if I ate very little here, and all the wrong things, my stomach ulcer would recur and bleed again and they would have to move me to a normal hospital.

A patient down the hall was barking like a dog.

I tried to examine my position logically, if logic was possible. My mother had written me that she was off for her usual summer trip to Europe. Her letter was waiting for me when I arrived at the hospital; also one from my brother saying he was going to Hawaii. My husband had taken the children to Martha's Vineyard, the place I love more than any other in the world. "Dear God, am I alone."

I felt completely abandoned. I knew none of my family could really help me by staying around, and I was aware that life must go on, but I did wish they were closer; they were so far away physically, in addition to being separated from me by the chasm between rationality and irrationality.

From a letter that a member of my family wrote to

me, one sentence stood out in my mind: "I'm sure you'll be your old smiling self again in no time." I was not so sure. Where was this self?

I would have to hide whatever I wrote in this place; furthermore, I would, little by little, hide bits of clothing during the day, under the mattress and other places, so that if I escaped I would not have to be dressed only in a nightgown.

"By God, I'll steal to get fifteen cents, if I ever see a chance to make a phone call. Some attendant must leave a purse or a wallet unwatched sometime or other."

The patient down the hall had stopped barking. What had they done, thrown her a bone?

I heard what must be a kennel of hounds quite far away. The dogs appeared to be howling and baying at the moon. I thought of long ago, when my father and I used to get up before sunrise and go fox hunting or "cubbing" in the early fall. He would help me tie my stock, and we would have breakfast together. Except for us, the whole house would be asleep, which was an added excitement. It would still be dark, and the dew would be on the ground. You could smell the horses, the first frosty tang of cold air, and the leather smell of saddles and bridles. The horses would sneeze, and paw the ground, and chomp on their bits, and their breath and yours would rise in the air like smoke. The hounds would be all excited when they were let loose, and yelp as the day began to break.

The memory hurt with such a poignant hurt. I think I realized, for the first time, with my heart, that my father was dead. Although he had died many months ago, I had known it only with my mind, as a fact, but not completely with my feelings. He, more than anyone else, would have understood something of what was happening to me. It had never been brought home to me so thoroughly and finally that he could help me no longer, ever again. Due to my parents' divorce, I had never seen enough of him; therein lay a big part of my grief.

In a rage I shouted, "How could you leave me and desert me again like this? I need you more than I've ever needed you before."

After a while my anger and grief subsided and I thought, "No, thank God, he has been spared seeing his daughter go through a mental illness and an unhappy marriage. I am grateful he cannot see me here as I am, because he would have blamed himself somehow, and suffered over it. All I could do was to remember how life was once, compare it with how it was now, and agonize because it would never be wonderful again. I thought, "I will be like this forever. Please, God, let me not lie here waiting for the deep and dreamless sleep I know will never come, and let me not feel my brain, shifting back and forth in my head from gear to gear, unstoppable and without cessation.

"If I should sleep, don't let me wake up in horror, as if there had been an explosion inside my head, so that I lie in bed afraid to move, terrified of my fragmented self. Oh, God, where is the morphine for the mind?"

My first morning: A loud bell, literally right outside my window, and seemingly inside my head, rang at 7:30. Its merciless clang made me shudder. I couldn't bear loud noises; just then all my nerves felt raw and exposed.

The door was unlocked, and in walked Miss Scotch

Burr with a breakfast tray. Apparently I was indeed not to be let out of my room.

"I can't drink coffee," I said meekly.

"Well, what do ye want?" she asked.

"Hot milk, please."

"It won't be hot, but you'll get the milk."

"My poor ulcer," I thought.

After breakfast, a doctor, quite an old man, came into my room and said he had just talked to my doctor at home (the one who sent me here), who wanted to know how I was getting along. This fool told him I was getting along beautifully and adjusting very well. I could have killed him on the spot. How dare he tell my doctor such a lie, and why wasn't I allowed to speak for myself about how I was doing? This was the epitome of betrayal and frustration. This man hadn't even seen me until this very moment.

I asked politely, "Why wasn't I allowed to talk to him?"

The doctor answered, "We think it is better for you not to just now."

"No wonder you do, you traitor and hypocrite," I thought; "you know damn well if my doctor knew how I felt, he would help me get out of here." The frightening part was that he was too sick to get up here to see for himself, or to see me. He had cancer. I was sure he would come to see for himself if he were not so sick. I trusted him implicitly, and if he felt the place was wrong for me, he would move me to another hospital.

The head of the hospital came in and gave me a peppy little lecture on how your first day here was like your first day at camp—you have to adjust, etc. I never went to camp, but if it's like this, God help those hundreds of shiny, eager little faces you see in Grand Central Station every July.

I asked, "Is your room locked at camp?"

He answered, "We don't want you to see the rest of the patients yet—they may be a shock to you."

I said, "They'll be just as much of a shock three days from now as today. I have to face them sometime—I might as well get shocked early as late. What's the matter with them, do they have two heads or something? After all, I am sick too."

The doctor answered, "Most of them are a lot sicker than you."

I said, "In that case, I must be in the wrong place. Locking me up is driving me wild, and I am imagining a lot worse things than I could possibly see."

"You may have a point; we'll see."

I asked, "Who is going to be my doctor?"

"He'll be here later. He's a nice young man who comes over from a big hospital near here three times a week to help out. Meanwhile, can we do anything for you?"

"Yes, let me out of this damn rat run."

Exit head of camp, locking the door behind him.

A fair-haired, youngish nurse came in to see me. She seemed gentle and nice, sympathetic and understanding. We had a long talk. She asked me how I felt about the place.

I answered, "So far, my one idea is to run away. I don't see why I'm locked in my room."

She said, "Have patience, and cooperate."

Thus far I could not very well not cooperate.

An occasional word from a friendly, interested, kind person like this nurse gets through to your emotions and reaches behind and beyond your fears.

My personal doctor came to see me after lunch, in my room, and I have seldom taken such an intense dislike to anyone on sight. To begin with, he was very young, which gave me no sense of confidence. He seemed cocky. No empathy here, I feared.

His first remark was, "Well! You've certainly gone over the line."

This was guaranteed to get us off to a grand start. Even if you know you have gone over the line, you don't like to be reminded of it in quite such terms.

"If this squirt wants a fight, he'll get one," I said to myself.

I didn't say anything.

"I asked you a question."

"You did not ask me a question—you made a very unkind statement. As you put it so well, I have indeed crossed the line, and I can't seem to get up quite enough speed to get off the ground to get back on the right side."

"Your marriage is not a good one, is it? I could tell it wasn't last night, when you were admitted. I was in the office. Did you see me?"

I answered, "I didn't see anybody or anything. On the other hand, I see no way in which you could size up my marriage, since I never opened my mouth." And, I thought, "You're an overpositive little son-of-a-bitch, that's what you are."

"I could tell there was tension between you and your husband."

I said, "The circumstances sort of called for tension, don't you think? Getting signed into a nut house is not exactly relaxing for anyone."

"I would prefer you not to refer to this place as a nut house. What do you think bothers you most?"

"Right now, being here."

"Then what brought you here?"

I did some rapid mental calculations. I did not like this man, I doubted if I was going to trust him, and I hoped to God I wasn't going to be here long. I had to make sure of one thing, and that was that my husband would be allowed to visit me, so that somehow I could make him understand that it was imperative to get me out of here. I thought, "I'll play the marriage as being happy, and drag in a lot of other possible factors that may have contributed to my breakdown."

I said, "I came here because I was obsessed with the idea that I had to commit suicide, even though I didn't want to. Also I was having delusions. In other words, I couldn't and cannot function."

"Did you like the doctor who took care of you before you came here?"

"I loved him."

"What are some of the factors that you think may have contributed to your acute depression?"

I answered, "My father's death, my brother's mental illness, my ulcer. I will think of a lot more causes if you give me time."

"Well," he said, getting up, "you do some thinking. We'll get to the bottom of this."

"Not on your tintype," I thought; "not you, and not here."

I asked, "When will I see you again?"

"We don't tell our patients that sort of thing."

"That's unnecessarily cruel," I shouted in a rage. "I simply want the reassurance that I *will* see you; something tangible and positive to hang my hat on."

"You'll have to get over being so dependent."

"I know, but this is a tough time to start. Why can't you tell me just for now?"

"I can, but I won't."

"Then I'll leave."

"No, you can't."

Is he right, or am I right? I am terrified–I don't know what I signed.

He closed the door and locked it. I leaned against it, my heart beating in my throat and choking me. This was an enemy, not a friend. I thought, "How can he help to make me well? He is as threatening as everything and everybody else here, and he is unsympathetic, cold, and totally uncaring. If he can make snap judgments, so can I.

"Out of my muddled mind, I'll have to concoct reasons that will appear to have brought on my illness until I can see my husband and get out of here. Above all, I must not mention our marriage, because I may not be allowed to see my husband."

The doctor stuck his head back in the room (without knocking, I might say, but I guess he figured I would hear the key turn–still, a little courtesy makes you feel less like an animal). "Incidentally," he said, "that nurse you talked to said you were contemplating running away. I wouldn't advocate trying it."

"Oh, really," I replied. "Anyway, there are other ways of getting out of here."

I was trying to bolster up my courage. I did not think there were other ways of getting out.

He said, "You can't get out of here until you are well, and that's up to us to decide."

"Oh, no. I can get out of here—there are other places I can go to," I shouted in desperation.

He closed and locked the door again. He had succeeded in terrifying me. He left me dripping with sweat, limp and shaking.

I had been knifed in the back by that nurse; I had thought she was my friend. Why did she repeat what I said about wanting to run away? Reasonably, I knew it was part of her duty to pass on information such as I gave her; she had to. I still liked her, and she would remain a friend, but I would just keep in mind constantly the fact that I could not trust anyone in this place—not anyone.

I was terrified of shock treatment because my brother had said it was awful. He had been hospitalized some years before, when the therapy was in a crude state; it's been much refined since. But I did not know that then. I did not know if they used it here, or gave it. I didn't dare ask, in case they were contemplating it.

I turned on my radio-phonograph and heard Jacques Frey's voice introducing some music. I knew Jacques Frey. Once we had played the piano together at a party, when I was normal and happy. I switched off the machine. The memories hurt too much to bear.

I could not read. I could not concentrate, and the words swam all over the page like a mass of amoebas under a microscope.

A pleasant book did not get through to me, not

even my beloved shell books which I had collected, along with shells, all my life. The shells I love so much just looked like "things" right then. I knew, as I looked at them, that what first drew me to them was the miracle of their infinite variety, shape, and color, but now none of this showed.

I kept trying to draw my room. Either I was drunk or it was a crazy-house Coney Island-type room. "I'm in a crazy house, so maybe the room is crazy too. I'm crazy, and I'm in a crazy house," I thought.

I moved some more clothes to my hideaway under the mattress. When they locked my clothes up each night, I felt that the clothes I had hidden were a little more free, and that made me more free too. If they ever turned the mattress over, it would be too bad for me, but they did not seem to get around to doing it.

There was a swimming pool outside my window. One evening one of the staff and his wife and little children, a boy and a girl, were using the pool. The happy shouts of "Mummy, look at me," were more than I could bear. "I had all this once too, dear God; have I lost it forever?" I asked myself.

I shut myself up in the bathroom and blocked my ears–that's where they found me when the dinner bell rang. If they thought I was crazy sitting in a corner of the bathroom with my hands over my ears, they were right. For once they didn't ask me what I was doing.

After dinner, an elderly Viennese doctor came in to "chat" with me, and he talked about the ups and downs of life, and how things go in cycles.

His accent in English was atrocious, so we ended by talking in French.

I am sure he meant to be kind, but obviously he thought I was queer because I was in this place. The odd thing is that I thought he was queer too.

Another doctor who came in to see me wore a patch over one eye. Just then physical deformities repelled me, and I didn't think I could look at him if I were his patient.

I did not know why doctors kept popping in, unless it was to make sure that I had not gone up in smoke.

A few days later the first person I had met there who made any real sense came into my room. She was the occupational therapist—a term I've always hated. She was kind, interested, enthusiastic, full of ideas, and intelligent. She had hit a gold mine in me, who all my life have loved doing work with my hands—knitting, needlework, sewing, playing the piano, making shell designs, painting. I told her that they had taken away my knitting and tapestry needles, all of my needles, in fact, and my little scissors. She said she would bring me some sewing and a hooked rug I could work on. I was elated.

True to her word, she brought some sewing, and a hooked rug to start on. She also brought a very little pair of scissors and asked, "Do you think I can trust you with these?"

I answered, "Do *you* think so? I am no longer sure myself. I don't think I'd take these scissors if I thought they could hurt me. I don't really want to do myself harm; that's why I asked for help."

She said, "If you leave the door open while you are using them—"

"Leave the door open?" I blurted out. "I wish to God *they'd* leave it open."

"Well, promise to turn the scissors in at night."

"They'll *take* them away."

She looked at me so kindly and said, "I'll ask them not to."

"Look, don't worry," I said, "if I were thinking of severing my jugular vein, whether the door is open or shut matters not one whit, since the job is silent; but it would be messy and lengthy with these little blunt things, and an awful lot of trouble. I'm not even quite sure where my jugular vein is."

She smiled and left me.

I worked happily all day, and in the late afternoon my new friend brought me some tiles to paint, which she said we could bake in the oven later on. We talked for a long time while I worked.

She remarked, "You know, you go at your work too hard, too fast, too desperately–and too frenetically."

"I guess I do, but it's the way I feel. Time stands still for me now, it is endless, and yet if I have something to do, I get the sense that there will not be time enough to finish it, or that someone will stop me from finishing it, or take it away from me. It's as if I were driven by demons to get it done."

She said, "You are an intelligent person, and you will help yourself to get well quickly."

"You know," I answered, "you're the first person who has mentioned intelligence versus nonintelligence, instead of sanity versus insanity. You make me feel like a human being. I will do everything to get well, because I want to more than anything else in the world, and I will help myself, but the setup here really gets me."

"Give it a try," she said as she got up to leave.

I was grateful. I should not forget her.

One day they saw fit to spring me from my room. I don't know why I felt as if I had been handed the world on a platter. I ran out of my room like a happy idiot, as if I were going to a party.

My first meal in the dining room was quite unbelievable. No one introduced anyone to anyone—one just sat and looked at one's plate. Not one single person said one word. I kept thinking, "This can't go on. No matter how withdrawn you feel, you have to *try* to talk." I heard one of the waitresses address one of the patients as Mrs. McHenry.

I exclaimed, "Oh, I wonder if you are any relation to the McHenrys who were on the *Andrea Doria* with us when she was rammed and sunk by the *Stockholm.*"

She answered, "Yes, we're related."

That was the end of that.

I noticed one of the doctors eating alone at a table in the corner of the dining room and I thought, "I am going to make a great 'thing' out of this *Andrea Doria* episode. This doctor will probably tell my doctor that the incident preys on my mind, and then it will appear to be a main reason for my illness." I regaled the assembled tablemates with every gory detail I could remember of the shipwreck, adding a good many exaggerations about what it had done to my nerves permanently (as a matter of fact, it had scared the hell out of me), hoping the doctor was sopping it all up with his soup.

After lunch I played the most extraordinary game of pool, or billiards. Some redheaded woman grabbed my arm as we were leaving the dining room and steered me toward the pool table, set up the balls, and handed me my cue, with never a word. It was like two small children playing, both in the same game, yet neither one paying any attention to what the other one is doing—never really competing. The woman never waited for my turn, so I saw no point in waiting for hers. I just took a turn whenever I felt like it. Redhead ran up the score according to her way of thinking, and I did not bother to argue. I had always detested the game anyway. We then tried Ping-Pong with a dented ball, which, thank God, got lost very soon under an immovable sofa. The redhead just walked off. Each person seemed to live alone in his own particular madness here—herded in a group, yet alone.

There was a rule that you could not discuss what was wrong with you, so it left very little to talk about.

I thought that after a certain amount of time here, I would look at my dinner plate all through the meal in silence too. Your former life was either too painful to talk about because you missed it so, or it was too remote—it was not even part of you anymore, except that it had a capacity to hurt unbearably when you heard children mentioned, or things you had seen done and loved in times past.

A new patient came in before dinner, and I knew her. We had been friends at Martha's Vineyard. How strange it felt to meet a friend here; it made me feel naked. She talked some and was most discouraging. She had been to several institutions, and said they were all awful, and she was getting worse and worse. When I asked after her family, she said her husband and children had abandoned her. She said she would like the lack of freedom here, from what she could see, because it might make her better. I said that I would like the free place she had described which she had just left, and asked her where it was, and what was its name. She told me, and I decided to aim at getting there. She was at my table at dinner but did not talk anymore, and after a while I gave up. Mrs. McHenry was missing. Someone said she had been to the dentist to have a tooth pulled and that the dentist was a butcher. That was a cheery note. My gums had been bleeding for days, but I certainly would not mention it to anybody.

After dinner, things picked up a bit. The lady who had said the dentist was a butcher, the redheaded one, and a frightened little wraith of a woman whom I had seen in the dining room (she appeared never to eat) suggested we play bridge. I grabbed this opportunity like a drowning man grabs a piece of driftwood—anything not to go back to my room, anything to make a few hours pass more quickly.

The wraith started to talk after the first hand was dealt, and she never stopped thereafter. It was the first time I had ever heard her utter so much as a word. We tried to play bridge around and between her remarks. It was truly the Mad Hatter's tea party—you never knew from one moment to the next how many were going to be at the table. I bid, and redhead, whose turn it was, was, as always, missing, so my partner, the wraith, went chasing around after her to tell her my bid. Wraith bid almost anything she wanted, because her partner was in a perpetual brown study over her teeth (she was the dentist-hater) and responded not at all. At any rate, wraith's bid had nothing to do with either her partner's or her opponents'. For a while we played a bastard form of three-handed bridge. After a bit, since our number was reduced to two, the woman who did not like the dentist started to play some weird kind of solitaire with her bridge hand, a cross between honeymoon bridge and pounce. I saw that her plans didn't include me, so I picked up the other pack of cards and played a form of solitaire of my own. In the middle of my game, up popped redhead behind me, and shouted, "Two spades." Then off she hopped, looking exactly like the white rabbit. All that was lacking were the dormouse and the teapot. The wraith came back to the table and said, "I never told you her bid." "Oh, you must have," I replied, "because redhead bid three hearts." "Oh, fine," said the wraith, "then I can bid two no-trump." She then played two no-trump with a mixture of hands left on the table by redhead and me. She went down four or five tricks, I think, and apologized profusely to me, her erstwhile partner. "Forget it," I said; "there are no score pads or pencils anyway, so it really doesn't matter. We aren't playing for money, because none of us has any money." "Oh, that doesn't matter," she said; "I owe someone here four thousand dollars." If the poor thing ever gets out of here, her creditors will be waiting at the gate.

I went back to my room, and for the first time

since I came to this place, I really laughed about something. I laughed till I hurt, but then the laughter turned to tears. After all, I was no visitor here. I was part and parcel of the place and those people. I believed they were, on the whole, much sicker than I was, or was that what everyone thought about everyone else? "No," I thought, "the others really are sicker than I am."

A girl came by the open door of my room and said she was going to make a phone call—you had to have been there months to earn that privilege. How I envied her! I wanted to follow her. Going to the movies was considered highly rewarding, too.

I thought of that thick, heavy, dark, wooden, bolted door downstairs. Once, long ago, it must have been a beautiful door, and this house must have been a beautiful house, and maybe it was even a happy one.

The girl who made the phone call came back. She was very tall and her head shook at times. She lived on the floor above me and seemed to have been there for a long long time. I thought she resented me for having been given the room she had had for years.

What utterly defeated me about the place was that all the other inmates, or patients, as we were euphemistically called, seemed to have given up. When I said, "I'm going to get well, and get out quickly," they all laughed or scoffed and said, "Oh, yes, we thought that too, but don't kid yourself."

I did an awful thing. I stole twenty-five cents, two dimes and a nickel, from the purse of one of the aides who was called out of the room while she was making my bed. I felt that if I should manage to escape, I would have to make a phone call ultimately. I could not stagger down the parkway back to New York, with police probably alerted.

Actually, hating the place, and my doctor, and a good part of the staff, was practically a pastime in itself. I hated the unfairness of it all. I was no longer afraid of killing myself. I suppose for one thing it was impossible, but I think it was more because I was obsessed with hating something besides myself. I got into blind panics of claustrophobia, but I did not think of killing myself—only of escaping.

It was frustrating that there was no way of telling people on the outside my real feelings about the place, and how much I would like a chance to try another hospital. My letters were returned to me if "they" did not like what I had written, and I refused to write what was not true—it was not worth writing.

I even tried writing to my sister in French, but they returned that letter in a hurry. Actually, I said nothing to her except that I was fine, and the weather was lovely, and how were the children. I wanted to see if "they" were energetic enough to have it translated, in which case it would have gone through, because it contained nothing critical.

I thought this mail censoring was the final indignity and invasion of my rights. "They" said, "You might upset people on the outside." I was not going to upset my doctor or my lawyer—that was a feeble excuse.

My gums were bleeding very badly, but I would not tell anyone. The dentist sounded like a monster, and who was going to believe me in my present state when I said I was allergic to novocaine? How could I get hold of some vitamin C? They never gave you any juices here. Less petunias and more oranges and lemons were needed—but of course visitors wouldn't see the oranges and lemons.

I went to my room and cried today because the nurse I liked so much left for good. She never even said "Good-bye." My doctor unfortunately found me crying.

"Why are you crying?" he asked.

I answered, "Because I liked the nurse who left; she seemed to be my only friend, and I feel deserted."

"We don't encourage personal relationships here, you know."

"You're telling me! What are you supposed to latch on to in this dump?"

"I'm sorry you feel it's a dump."

"Well, it's a very swell dump, I'll say that, petunia beds and all, but I hate it because it's all for show, from the polished locked front door to the waxed floors, so that the visitors will say, 'What lovely surroundings.' But they don't see its lack of heart. You could have a lot less petunias and floor wax, and a lot more warmth."

"You can't have heart with these cases."

"These cases—that's typical! Everyone is just another case. Maybe I'm different from the lady down the hall who barks, maybe she doesn't need any heart—I do. Let me tell you, the doctor I had before I came here had a heart, and he used it, and it made one hell of a difference."

Doctor: "Why didn't you stay with him?"

"Because he's dying of cancer, that's why, and also I knew I needed protection from myself—but there is protection and protection, and I don't want the kind I get here. If I could talk to my own doctor on the outside, he'd put me in some other place, where I'd be a lot happier."

"Well, you can't talk to him. I tell you that personal attachments are misplaced in these situations, so it is just as well that the nurse you liked so much has left, and you have another doctor."

"Don't worry, I'm not contemplating getting attached to you, so the problem won't exist." (I had better not tell him I like the occupational therapist, I guess, or that one remaining relationship will have to go too.)

"I hear you were on the *Andrea Doria*," said the doctor.

"Oh," said I, "how did you hear that?"

"You were overheard discussing it. Did the experience bother you much?"

"Bother me! You make it sound like a mosquito annoying someone. You're damn right it bothered me; in fact, it terrified me, and I'll guarantee you it terrified everyone else just as much, if not worse."

"Did you panic?"

"Inside yes, outside no. We had our children with us."

"Do you think it's responsible for your illness?"

"Oh, yes, I'm sure it is, that and my father dying shortly after it—these were all profound shocks to me."

"Are you sure there's nothing else? Was that enough to make you suicidal?"

"Evidently."

"I want to discuss your marriage. I noticed some hostility the night–"

"You already told me that. My marriage is fine, fine." (For God's sake, I've got to seem to get along well enough with my husband so he will be allowed to visit–otherwise I'll be here for life.)

"I don't feel you are telling me everything, or giving much. Until you change your attitude, we will get nowhere."

"I don't think we're on the same wavelength myself. With some people you can give, but with others you can't. You must trust someone completely to give out a lot."

"And you don't trust me?"

"No, not really."

"Why not?"

"I just don't. I can't explain it. Perhaps I could change doctors." (That's a bit of bravado; I don't think I'd like old Vienna or patch-eye either.)

"No, that's not the answer. You're absolutely wrong. We must work together."

(That's what you think. Find something to babble about, you idiot, something that can be made to look as if it disturbed you very much–anything except your marriage. My sister's marriage, that'll throw him. She's married to a Negro, it's unusual, at any rate, and although it doesn't bother me anymore, I can say it does.)

We discussed this for a while. Before he left, I asked him, "Why aren't the patients allowed to work in the garden?"

"Because we like to have it look tidy."

"I could help to keep it tidy."

"Why do you want to?"

"Because it's a good form of exercise, and I would just like to feel the soil."

"Well, we can't allow it," he said as he left.

I supposed if I said I hated working in the garden, that's exactly what they would have me doing, all day every day.

I would not tell this doctor why I felt so trapped because I knew why already. Meanwhile I could only pray that my husband would have the sympathy and understanding to get me out of here, regardless of how we got on, and find a better place for me.

It was funny how little I missed cigarettes, liquor, small treats. There did not seem to be enough of me left to even have any bad habits.

They had a theory that each patient should drink eight glasses of water a day. Why eight? Why not seven, or nine? I forgot to drink my glass regularly, so I ended up drinking six or seven at once. Considering they locked the bathrooms at night, this seemed to me to be a particularly inept theory.

The Head Man strutted around the place like Napoleon, minus his tricorne hat. He never addressed a patient. It did not cost much to say, "Hello, how are you?" Who did he think he was?

Weekends were unbearable. There was no occupational therapy, and you did an awful lot of sitting alone in your room. The days were endless and forlorn, and there was too much idle time for terrors to move in.

Sundays some of the patients had visitors, but not I. I had not had enough time to "adjust" yet. If I ever adjusted to the place, God help me.

I just sat, frozen, in my chair in my room.

I felt like a bird that flew into our greenhouse once. It beat itself to death against the glass because it could not find any exit, and we could never catch it to help it get out. Where were the exits here, and how keen were they to help you use them?

I picked up my hooked rug and went at it with a vengeance.

Monday was a typical day, and I thanked God it had some kind of schedule—even if I did not like the schedule.

After breakfast we were led, and I mean led, to the occupational-therapy building, where the teacher was busy unlocking all the tools. I was in the process of hammering what the therapist said was going to be an ashtray, out of a piece of metal. I could not stand the noise I made; it hurt my ears and my whole head—in fact, my whole body. Maybe the therapist thought I'd hammer out my hostility or something. I like to finish anything I start, out of pride, but I did not think I could stick this out.

Some of the other patients opened up a bit during occupational-therapy sessions. They kept scoffing at me when I said I was going to get well and I was going to get out of here or any other place I had to go, fast. They all said, "Look at us." I looked at them, and I panicked, but I honestly did think they were sicker than I was. They showed no desire to communicate or to improve.

After occupational therapy, we spent an hour

alone in our rooms; then came lunch, and the usual abysmal silence and staring at plates. Then we had what was supposed to be a nap, or a silent period in our rooms. As far as I am concerned, the whole day was a silent period.

Then we went for a walk. There were some very nice high-school kids who volunteered their services in the summer to take patients for walks. I couldn't help thinking of the irony of this—the girl who took me for walks was younger than my eldest daughter, and here she was telling me what to do.

I had a tremendous obsession about bees, since I had once almost died from a sting. I had been allowed to keep a gold locket, which hung on a chain around my neck, with pills in it, in case I did get stung—one pill to swallow, and one to put under my tongue so my throat would not close off. I did not dare walk in the orchard, where there was clover, because there are often bees where there is clover, so I stayed on the paths.

At one point during a walk I had to go to the bathroom. I saw the high-school girl write something in a little notebook. "Good God," I thought, "is this going on my record too—incontinence or something?" If I had written down the names of all my friends who had to go to the bathroom on walks, picnics, etc., and they were considered queer because of it, mental hospitals would be overflowing, literally. The trouble was everything you did was made to look queer and "uncontrolled."

After our walks we were taken to the swimming pool for a supervised swim. One day I left my locket at the edge of the pool, and "they" would not let me go back and look for it after I had gone back to my room and discovered its loss. I asked if "they" would please look for it, and "they" said yes, but I think "they" couldn't have looked very hard, because "they" didn't find it, and I knew just where I had left it. I did not dare go for a walk at all then, but I knew I would be forced to. I was beginning to see bees everywhere, swarming all over the walls. I asked if "they" would give me the same pills to carry in a little box in my pocket—but not "they." "They" said if a bee should sting me that I could get back from anywhere I happened to be in time to get treatment. How dumb could "they" get? "They" must realize how appallingly fast the reaction to a bee sting can be—it is a matter of minutes. I think they were cruel and enjoyed frightening me.

How strange to want to be dead, even to the extent of contemplating killing yourself, on the one hand, and on the other, to be terrified of dying from a bee sting.

One afternoon I developed a better plan of escape than I had thought of before. Outside my room, across the hall, was a balcony with a locked screen door that opened onto some steps that went down to the garden and to the path that led to the swimming pool. Several times I had noticed a gardener's truck parked near the bottom of the steps. Suppose I were able to force the screen door of the balcony—it looked flimsy—and grab that truck? The gardener probably left his keys in it, and assuming it did not have some complicated gear shift which I might not be able to work, I might be able to get away.

I might have to escape in my bathing suit, because I would try this plan the minute after they brought me back to my room from the pool, when they leave you alone for a few minutes. People in bathing suits have been seen driving cars without arousing any suspicion, I thought. If I could get to a gas station with my stolen quarter and make a phone call, would I arouse suspicion? I could flounder around the woods and attempt to find a friend of mine who lived about a mile from here, or I could even, perhaps, ask the way along the road. Would my friend turn me in if I showed up hysterical and disheveled? I think she'd give me the chance to call home at least, or my lawyer. The only thing was, if I failed, I knew "they" would think I was twice as crazy, and I might just make things worse, although that seemed impossible.

At night we had our usual dismal dinner, and I played Ping-Pong. It seems to be the only game someone will stick to for any length of time. I thought I was good at Ping-Pong, but the balls were all shaped like eggs and the angles of the bounce were unusual.

After lights were out, I sneaked to the head of the stairs to see if the nurse on duty at the desk had left her post temporarily. I looked and looked at the mahogany front door. It was hopeless to try to get out that way.

I brooded about this place I was in. Many years before, my brother had tried to run away from school because he was miserable and confused about my parents' divorce. He was put, at the school's advice, in this hospital. I went to see him. He was the only child there. He was weaving a basket. I knew it was a place where people were "different." I thought, "If this happens to you when you make a mistake or do something bad or disobedient, who is there ever to stand behind you and protect you and love you when you most need it? No one. Only when you are good, and stick to the rules, and don't make any trouble will you be accepted and loved." How ironic it was that he should have been sent to the same hospital I was in now. If I were superstitious, I would say that a shadow had fallen across my life then, that caught me in its darkness years later.

I played tennis with the tall girl who had been there so long. My body was as weak and uncoordinated as my mind was, and it annoyed me, because I can play tennis well. My muscles just did not seem to get the message. We were supervised while we played, and this irked me. In the middle of the game, I thought I heard a Mercedes horn. I dropped my tennis racquet and ran back to the main house, my heart pounding and my hopes high. I thought it was my husband come to fetch me, maybe, but it was someone else's Mercedes. I went back to the court with a sinking heart. The tall girl won two sets and was as delighted as if she had won at Forest Hills. I can be competitive too, but here and now I simply don't care one way or another. This girl has made this place her world, and I wouldn't. As we were leaving the court, two men appeared and asked us to play mixed doubles. I hadn't even known there were men patients here. I guessed they were segregated. I wondered if they had tea dances once a month; how monstrous to contemplate. No woman could possibly make up her face here, and offhand, it really didn't look as if the men would be worth it if she could.

I went to the hairdresser, because everyone else went. The hairdresser, a man, asked me how I wanted my hair done. I said I didn't care. He lifted my chin up and said, "But you must care. Look at yourself in the mirror; you look pretty, and we must make you prettier." I asked, "What for?"

He answered, "Because it's good for you to look your best. First of all, we'll have a haircut, and then I'll do something beautiful—you'll see." I buried my head in a magazine, not one word of which I absorbed, because I simply could not bring myself to look in a mirror.

When the hairdresser had finished, he said, "Now look. How lovely, no?" I looked, and I smiled. How long had it been since I had smiled, I wondered? My face looked entirely different with my hair nicely done, and a smile. "Are you pleased?" asked the hairdresser. "Yes, I am," I answered.

"Keep smiling," he said; "you are lovely when you smile."

"What is there to smile about here?" I asked. "I think if you smiled here you would look like the village idiot. I never see anyone else smile."

"I know," he said, "but try, and look at yourself more often until I see you next time. Is that a promise?"

"O.K.," I answered, "I'll trv."

I went back to my room and studied my face in the mirror. I just did not know myself.

In occupational therapy I was painting, and I loved

it. I was having some sport trying to confuse the people who were interpreting these paintings. If I felt frightened and really deeply depressed, I painted bright sunny scenes; if I felt a little better, I painted tunnels and labyrinths and dark, dark, dark, all over. In a way I was confusing myself by doing this, so I guess it was pretty stupid. I loved handling the paints, and I delighted in the smell of them, the turpentine, and the linseed oil.

One night one of the doctors asked me whether or not I'd like to go to the movies the next afternoon, or stay "home" and see my husband.

I said, with my heart pounding, "I want to see my husband, obviously."

"They don't want me to see him, the devils, because they are afraid I'll tell him something unfavorable about this place, and are they right!"

All night I was tormented about whether or not my husband would believe me. It all looked so nice, but it had no heart, no caring, no soul, no kindness, really, and everything good was external. I did not like my doctor—in fact, I hated him, and I did not trust him, but he might make a good impression on my husband. Considering the state of our marriage, and the fact that I wanted a separation and my husband did not, I was rather at his mercy. Also, when you are mentally ill, other people are inclined to believe what the doctors say, not what you say.

Next day my husband arrived with a bunch of flowers. He said, "The doctors tell me you are doing wonderfully, and will be out of here in a few weeks."

"That's a lie," I shouted; "they are a bunch of

hypocrites. They've been threatening me and telling me that they can keep me here as long as they want." Then I told him all the increased feelings of terror and claustrophobia, not to mention resentment, that the treatment here was giving me, and bless him, he promised to get me out. He promised to come back in the morning.

"You really promise—you mean this?" I asked. "You're not just calming down an overwrought nut?"

"No, I promise," he answered as he left.

"Thank God," I said, "you could have left me here to rot forever."

I spent that night lying rigid in the dark, trying not to think. If he didn't come back, I didn't know what I'd do.

Before breakfast the Head Man came marching in. My heart sank.

"I hear you don't like it here. What's wrong with the place?" he asked. He looked extremely angry, and he scared me.

I said, my voice quavering, "I'd like to try a different, more open place." Thump, thump went my heart. I was shaking all over, and felt faint, and I was having trouble breathing.

What do you say when everything is wrong? "I'm not making any progress here. I think the patients here are sicker than I am; in fact, I think most of them are chronically ill. This is bad for me. I don't like my doctor, either."

The Head Man said, "You won't like any other

place, either—you're a pretty sick girl, you know."

I screwed up my courage and said, "I'll have to see for myself about the other place, doctor. You just don't understand that I can't stand being locked up the way I am here. It is making me worse."

"You haven't given us a fair try; a lot of your trouble here is your own fault, you know."

"Oh, come on," I exploded in real anger, "I've been just as fair as you have; at least admit there's fault on both sides. I never fought my other doctor, and I want to get well. This place just isn't for me. I'd never get well here, and I might even get permanently worse. There's no use trying to explain how I feel to you."

He left the room and slammed the door.

Later on, after what seemed an eternity spent in agonizing doubt, my husband came to my room. He was just as frightened as I was.

"My God," he said. "I thought they really wouldn't let you go. They put up a hell of a fight, and really let me have it."

"Maybe you should have brought a lawyer," I commented. "I don't think either of us knows our legal rights. I signed myself in, and I think, only think, mind you, that I have the right to sign myself out."

Never have I packed so fast. We carried my bags down the stairs, where the doctors were lined up like a group of Charles Addams' butlers, each face more lugubrious and disapproving than the next. I felt like a naughty child being sent home from a birthday party for bad behavior. There were no words exchanged.

Oh, God, the relief of getting in our car, with the familiar smell of the leather. I turned down the windows; it was the first time in months I had really smelled fresh air, free air. I suddenly thought, "I forgot to pack my best tile that I was going to put in the oven, and my clothes under the mattress. But I wouldn't go back for them for anything in the world."

What an intoxicating feeling of liberty! We stopped at a Howard Johnson's, and I had a hamburger and a glass of milk. What a marvelous feeling to have some money to pay for them. Then and there I mailed a quarter to the aide from whom I'd stolen twenty-five cents.

3

Interim Period

"I am grateful you took me out—you'll never know how grateful; you could have left me there to rot," I said to my husband.

Later that day we drove up to a lovely, cozy-looking cluster of buildings. A very attractive woman showed us around and then took me to my room.

"You won't lock me up, will you?" I asked.

"Heavens," she exclaimed, "we wouldn't know where to find the keys to any of the doors."

"You mean I can just come and go, in and out?"

"Absolutely," she said. "There are no restraints here; you can order a taxi and leave any time you want to."

I said, "I don't want to go, I just want to know that I can."

I got unpacked and settled, and then someone took me to see the director, who seemed very kind and sympathetic. He told me that in a day or so I would have a doctor assigned to me. My husband talked to the director, and then left to go home. Home, I thought with a pang; shall I ever go back there, normal and cured?

The luncheon gong rang, the kind they use on shipboard, and I went into the dining room. I was introduced to several people at the table to which I was taken, and had a delicious meal.

Several of the women at the table were complaining about the rule here that forbids the "patients" to wear shorts. I thought, what a funny thing to complain about—they could insist on my wearing long underwear today in July and I would not care, because here you are free.

After lunch I was taken to the crafts building and shown how to weave on a loom. I was delighted with this; it was something I had never tried before.

For dinner, everyone changed and dressed up a bit. After dinner I played bridge, a good game of bridge, with a young girl and two older men. I was drunk with happiness and liberty. The girl was pretty and young and gay and said she was here for a rest from her husband and children for a couple of weeks. She asked me why I was here. It was as if a cold hand had squeezed my heart. Suddenly I felt inferior, hideous, out of place, terrified, and trapped again. I excused myself from the table and ran to my room and sat on the bed with my heart pounding so hard that I could hardly breathe. I wondered who you could talk to here about feelings like this until you got your own doctor.

No one seems to have a care in the world here.

A nurse gave me a large sleeping pill and I slept for the first time in weeks—absolutely a knocked-out, dead-to-the-world sleep.

Next morning, it being Sunday, I wandered around feeling a bit lost, longing to go for a walk, but afraid to go by myself. I was annoyed and upset by this reaction, because I had resented so terribly the supervised walks at the other place. Here I was free to go, and could not screw up my courage to do so. Finally I joined two other girls and we walked across the grounds to the main road. There I panicked and ran all the way back to my room.

I found the nice woman who had shown me around the day before and blurted out my terror to her. She asked if I would like a nurse assigned to me for a while, until I got acclimated. I said I'd feel queer if I had a nurse, because no one else had one. She said that many people had a nurse in the beginning, and by tomorrow she would see that I had one.

"Really," I thought, "what is the matter with me, asking for a nurse—I, who wanted to be free? Well, maybe I'll feel better in a few days."

One night I tried going to the movies with a group in a taxi. I had no idea what went on on the screen. Halfway through the movie I had to run out. I stood out in the street in front of the theater, hanging on to a lamppost, not knowing what to do, and panting as if I had run a mile. One of the women who had been in the taxi with me came out and asked if I was all right. I answered, "I don't know what's wrong, but I can't go back in there, and I can't stay here either."

She asked, "Would you like me to take you back to the sanitarium?" I burst into tears and said, "Yes, if you wouldn't mind. I'm so sorry to ruin your fun."

"It's nothing," she answered; "it's a lousy movie anyway. Didn't you think so?"

"Yes," I answered. I had no idea what movie we had seen.

All night a voice kept at me: "You're going to kill yourself." That hated voice was back.

I met my doctor; he seems sympathetic, gentle, and kind. I tried to explain my panic to him, about being enclosed and the contradiction of being unable to bear to be unprotected and in the open, and my terror about being told to commit suicide by someone inside of me that wasn't me. He explained to me that someone as emotionally upset as I am can have very ambivalent feelings about freedom. I clutched on to that word "ambivalent," to help me understand my divided, crazy feelings.

The doctor said, "For a while we will just discuss your current feelings, and not delve around into the past. I'll give you some medicine, you will have your nurse, and I am going to give you some reading to do."

I left his office laden with reading material and some orders about doing physical exercises twice a day in my room.

My nurse, who was a sweet person, said, "I'm just here when you want me. I don't want to intrude on your privacy in any way. If you want to be alone, or to do things alone, just say so. If you want me, I am here."

I had a cheery little room. I sat down at the desk

and tried to study my reading assignment. I thought some of it was very uplifting, but I couldn't absorb it and apply it to me. In my mind I knew that what the words said was good and helpful, but I couldn't really concentrate on them, and my vision was blurred. I tried my sitting-up exercises, which I vowed to do regularly.

I asked the nurse to take me to the crafts building. Everything went wrong in my weaving; the bobbins got in a fearful tangle, and I was reduced to tears. One of the teachers comforted me and said, "Let me show you how to tool a leather belt today; I think you'll get more pleasure out of that." I did indeed get more pleasure, except that my hands shook, and I didn't do a very good job on the belt either.

At lunch lobster was served, to which I am violently allergic, and I was terrified that I would be made to eat it. Instead, when I said, "No, thank you," the waitress asked, "Would you like an omelet?" I was so bowled over by being given this choice that I could hardly believe my ears.

I was troubled about my relationship with my doctor. I liked him very much, but I simply couldn't discuss my reading with him, because I hadn't absorbed it. I really wanted to shout at him, "Please, you don't understand. I am terrified that I am going to kill myself, and you must do something helpful right now. I can't wait, because I can't live with these feelings much longer." He tried to steer me away from this kind of talk, and I left the interviews with him more scared than ever, because we hadn't touched on anything real to me.

My nurse and I and two other women went to see a

play by Bernard Shaw put on by a summer-stock company. I cannot remember the name of the play. I was occupied with doing everything I could to fight down the desire to run out of the theater. I did not wish to be ashamed in front of the other two women who had come with us. In the intermission I rushed out and got a lemonade, and managed to get through the final act, dripping with perspiration, limp and exhausted, and hurting all over from sitting with my teeth and hands clenched.

Where will these inexplicable panics and nameless dreads lead me eventually? Was it possible that this lovely, comfortable, warm place, full of kind people, was too free for me, and that I was too sick to be here? God, I didn't want to leave, but this time I realized that I was the really sick one. I had trouble keeping up with the others. It was too hard to continually hide my horrible fears and to act and talk completely normally, when I lived in perpetual dread of running amok. Here, once more, I felt the abyss between the really sane and the not sane.

I was afraid that I would have to leave, and the prospect appalled me. Dear God, was there a place for me somewhere between the prison I was in and this too good, too free place, or was that horrible Head Man at the first sanitarium right? No, I wouldn't let him be right. There must be a place that would help me.

At the end of three weeks, sadly my doctor and I agreed that I was too sick for the freedom of this sanitarium.

I went home, but home was no longer home, and

everything and everyone in it were either terrifying, or totally unfamiliar. No one and nothing even looked the same, and this hurts more than anything. The people and things I loved were familiar, and yet had become removed and completely strange. I was miserable beyond words. Where could I go next? Where? What was left in the world for me to go to?

Autumn came, and the leaves fell with what was left of my courage.

My husband suggested that I have nurses at home and see a doctor once a day. I didn't think this would work. I felt I was a damaging influence on the children, and I could not bear to have them see me surrounded by nurses. Besides, home had become the most terrifying place of all. I couldn't understand why.

The doctor I had gone to first, whom I loved and trusted, had died of cancer. I thought of him always as invulnerable and strong. I didn't know whom to turn to now.

By December my husband found me a doctor. I couldn't even remember his name. I struggled to his office every day. He was trying a new drug. He talked to me, but I didn't hear what he said. I didn't know whether I answered or not. I wanted to ask him to save me, but I could no longer articulate my distress—in fact, I couldn't talk, except for monosyllables.

How many weeks went by this way? I knew nothing save pain, terror, total withdrawal, and the inability to move.

On Christmas day I tried so hard to be normal, for

the children. I could still talk to them, a little bit. I felt the children knew there was something queer and different about me. They were subdued and looked unhappy. I tried to react when they showed me their presents, but I don't think I succeeded. "Don't you like it, Mummy?" I heard from another world. The contrast between this Christmas and other ones hurts beyond belief; and I felt desolate.

I was there, but I was absent—a vacant, useless nothing.

The children would be better off without me.

After Christmas, we all went into New York to stay at our apartment. The children had some parties and dances they wanted to go to.

I watched them get dressed, one evening, for their parties—my son in his tuxedo, my daughters in their pretty dresses, and thought, "What has this to do with me?"

I was alone in the apartment at eleven at night. My husband had gone to pick up the girls at their dances, and my son had not yet come home.

I went out on the terrace of our apartment. There was a wall around it about chest-high. I thought, "The time has come to do away with myself. There is no use fighting anymore—there is no hope for me. This is the only way out. But the children, the children, what will become of them? Yet I must obliterate this horrible thing I have become."

I climbed up on the parapet of the wall, hanging on to the side of the building. "If I look down, I'm lost," I thought.

The telephone rang, and I stood there listening to it. I have never been able to let a phone go unanswered—to me it is like ignoring a person who is crying for help.

I climbed down off my perch, walked to the phone, and picked up the receiver. Whoever had been on the other end had hung up. I put the receiver down, ran to a closet, flung on a coat, rushed out of the apartment, and rang for the elevator. I went out into the icy cold and walked around and around the block. Finally I screwed up my courage to return to the apartment.

My son was home. He said, "You look awful, Mum. Can I help—get an aspirin or something?"

I laughed at the irony of an aspirin and said, "No, thank you, darling, but I'm glad you're here."

"Why, were you afraid to be alone?" he asked.

"Yes, I was. I just had a terrible dream."

"But you haven't been asleep—you just came in from outside."

"No, I guess I haven't been asleep, have I? Anyway, I'm glad to see you. Wasn't the dance any fun?"

"No, the girls were all messes."

What would he have thought, had he known what I had just been thinking and doing?

The next morning my stepmother telephoned me. She had a suggestion from a doctor friend of hers, about a doctor he knows who would be willing to treat me at the Presbyterian Medical Center at the Neurological Institute, which is an open hospital and yet affords some protection.

Again I packed a bag for God knows how long a stay in the hospital.

I took a taxi up to the Neurological Institute. I rode up in the elevator to the sixth floor, on which my room was. I walked into my room. The first thing I noticed was that the windows were not barred. You could open them with a crank, but you could not possibly jump out of them. This made me feel free and protected at the same time.

I asked the nurse who was admitting me if I could go out in the hall, or even out of the building if I wanted to. She said I could do whatever I wanted if I told someone at the desk where I was going and if I came back within a reasonable length of time. She left the room, and left me to my own devices.

I opened my door, went out in the hall, and walked to the elevator. I pressed the button, and when the elevator came, I rode up and down in it. Then I got off at the main floor, walked past the front desk with some trepidation, and out into the street. I walked for a block, turned around, and came back to the hospital. I got back in the elevator and rode down to the basement. There I found a vending machine with Hershey bars and other candies in it. I put some money in the slot and pushed the peanut-brittle button: out it came. I rang for the elevator again and got off at my floor.

I saw a pay-phone booth, entered it, and put a dime in the slot, and dialed the first number that came into my head. Evidently it was a "working" number, because a woman answered on the other end. I hung up. I couldn't very well tell her why I had dialed her number.

I returned to my room and started to undress, feeling frightfully pleased with myself. No one had taken away any of my things.

A nurse came in, and said, "Oh, you're back. You forgot to tell the person at the desk where you were going."

I was crestfallen. The nurse said, "Don't feel badly—everything is a bit confusing at first."

I said, "You are so nice about it. I don't really want to go out again. I only wanted to see if I could."

Everyone I meet here is friendly and kind. I like the atmosphere of the place. If my doctor is like everyone else here, I am bound to like him, and he will be able to help me.

I am on a "normal" floor, the nurses said, along with patients with slipped discs, spinal injuries, strokes, and so on.

Where was there a place on this green earth for someone who was afraid to be really free, yet couldn't stand to be locked up, couldn't go out, yet couldn't stay in, for fear of destroying herself—who was lost in limbo? I am not a prisoner here, but I am protected. Here they treat me like a consenting human being.

4

The "Good" Hospital

First day: I saw my doctor the first thing this morning. He knocked at the door, which impressed me. He was not wearing a white coat, and he looked so friendly and unclinical.

He asked, "Are you afraid?"

I answered, "A little, yes, but less than I have been so far." I took a quick glance at his eyes. They were kind.

"Why do you think you are less afraid?"

"I don't know. I think it is because I feel I can leave; but I don't really want to leave, you know. Also, I can't jump out of these windows, but I can open them. I've been cranking them all morning—they make me feel free, yet safe. I really want to stay and get well. I feel this is the end of the road. I have wandered so much, and been lost and alone for so long—over two years now. Please make me well."

The doctor drew up a chair next to my bed and sat down.

"Don't you worry," he said, "we will make you well. I will see you every day, and we will talk about your symptoms, your thoughts, your fears, and your delusions. I know how bad they can be, and how much they can hurt. I know you have gone through your history many times, but would you mind doing it once more? I have your records, you know, from your doctor who died, so you won't have to go back too far."

Once more I tried to put my illness into words.

The doctor listened and said, "I'm going to put you on certain medications. I know you are afraid of allergic reactions, so I will tell you exactly what each medication is, and we will start with small doses. Most of all, you want to sleep, don't you?"

"Oh, God, yes."

"I'll see to that. Would you like a television set?"

"Not yet; it scares me."

"I trust you, you know, not to leave without telling me first. You can call me on the telephone anytime. Trust *me*."

"Don't worry," I answered, "right now I don't even want to go down the hall to the solarium. I just like to have the door open so that I can hear everything that is going on on the floor. I do trust you."

"You and I will get you well," the doctor said with a smile and a pat. Then he left.

"Here," I thought, "is a man I can trust. He has a heart, and he will use it."

Another day: This morning the doctor asked me,

"Why did the other place, that first hospital you went to, frighten you so?"

I answered, "The other patients were really very sick there, sicker than I. They had vacant and unseeing eyes, and I felt they had been put away for keeps. They were silent and perpetually withdrawn; one kept barking, an old woman next to me. Everything was barred and locked, and they took away so many of my things, and locked my clothes up at night. I felt we were grouped together like animals, not individuals. I felt fenced in on every side, trapped forever, with no way to even communicate with anyone. The place gave me the feeling that I would never, never get out. I know that rules are necessary, but when you are not completely 'gone,' some of those rules make you feel so much worse than you are."

"You'll forget all this someday."

"Never," I answered. "Never in all my life. I wish you could do something about my nightmares about that place. The asleep ones, and the awake ones, and this churning brain of mine that will never be still for an instant—like a motor racing perpetually inside my head. I want to bang my head on the wall to make it keep still. That's why I seek oblivion."

"Be patient. The drugs you will be taking cannot perform miracles right away."

"Are you going to give me shock treatment? I am terrified of it. My brother said it was awful. The image I have of shock treatment is terrifying. I have never seen anyone having a shock treatment, but I see myself strapped down on a stretcher with wheels, and imagine my body arched so that the bones might break, and my eyes rolled back in my head like my son's when he had convulsions when he was a baby."

The doctor said, "I have not got that in mind for you. We want to see how these drugs work. Tell me, did you ever have any real depressions before this one?"

"Yes, I had quite bad ones after my children were born. It's funny, I was so happy to have a baby, and yet I went into very bad slumps a couple of weeks after each one was born. They got progressively worse with each child."

"Do you remember how long they lasted?"

"No, not really."

"Are you comfortable?" the doctor asked.

"Oh, yes, oh, yes, at last, at last."

I feel this man really cares. It's funny how you can feel it. I can even tease him a bit, and he laughs. Mainly he understands, in the fullest sense of the word. I feel I can at last pour out my whole heart and mind and soul. The stopper can finally be removed, and I can explode safely.

I do trust him. Oh, God, thank you, I do trust him. He doesn't take notes about what I say, at least not in front of me. That makes me feel more free to talk; and when he talks to me, his voice has the rare quality of complete reassurance.

The nurses are so nice, not officious and bossy, and they don't say, "How are *we* today?" They are kind and cheerful and sympathetic; so are the aides and the maid who cleans my room. She comes from a French island in the Caribbean, and we speak in French.

I often get up and open and shut the door, and stick my nose out in the hall, and poke into every nook and cranny of my room. They haven't taken anything of mine away. I have money, scissors, my clothes, my razor, cigarettes and matches.

I feel safe now, as if I were in a cocoon, and I feel as if I have some dignity.

Another day: I woke up feeling unusually low and panicky. I had the most tortured and incredible nightmares that stayed right on through the day with me.

The doctor came in and asked, "Did you sleep last night?"

"Yes and no. I will become a drug addict on top of everything else. I'll need more and more pills."

"Just for now, don't worry about that; you will not become an addict."

"I feel as if I were a bad mother. I feel I have abandoned my children—I feel terrible about it."

"They know you love them, don't they?"

"Oh, I hope so, I hope so, but they need constant reassurance, or else they will forget. All this must be hurting them; they must be puzzled. Why am I so cut off from them?"

"Soon they can come to see you. Some day they will understand, and all this will not hurt them as much as you imagine it may. It will make them more understanding. Can you tell me why you can't read or look at television? Why you just sit or lie huddled in bed or in a corner?"

"I don't know; I guess it's because it feels safe. I can't concentrate when I read, and the words are blurred. If some sentences do get through to me, I identify with everyone, in newspapers, on the radio, on television—all the bad things and people. I can't follow the good things and good people. You see, there is no me, particularly a good me, so I have become everyone bad."

"Do you think you could do something with your hands?"

"Yes, I want to. I'll get someone to bring me some knitting, some needlework, some puzzles, and some mosaic pieces to make a tabletop, and I can write. I write every day, you know. I write all my thoughts and everything people say. My writing is so peculiar, though, I can hardly read it."

"Good. We'll get you going on some creative things, and you keep writing."

"Do I have to hide what I write here?"

"Why should you have to?"

"In that other place—"

"You forget that other place. You aren't as frightened as when you came in here, are you?"

"No, not nearly. I still have terrible nightmares, and at night I am still very frightened, but in the daytime the nightmares usually stop. And I am beginning to feel a little bit safe. I don't think of killing myself nearly so often. You know, the thought comes unbidden and I am afraid of the thought, but the desire is almost gone. You won't make me leave here yet, will you?"

"You won't leave here until you feel you can face your life again as well as, if not better than before."

"Isn't it strange that I am asking you not to make

me leave when I would have done anything to break out of that other place? Why? Well, I'll answer my own question. I am free to go here but I don't want to. I am finding tender care and understanding."

Another day: Today my doctor asked me about my childhood, my health record, and any hereditary factors that "might have any bearing on my present illness."

I told him that I had been a rather lonely child, for several reasons.

I was brought up in enormous and isolated places, and in what seemed to me dark, cold, and somewhat frightening houses. I was taken care of by a string of nurses, governesses, and innumerable servants. My parents were remote, not only because of the long walks to their rooms, but also because they carried on a very busy social life and were frequently away on trips.

My older brother was sent to boarding school at the age of eight. My younger sister had an English nurse who wasn't on speaking terms with my French governess, and in the summers my brother had tutors who loathed them both, so life wasn't precisely what you would call congenial.

I think too much was expected of us by too many people. We felt we had to at least appear perfect. So many people told me that I should be like someone else, I ended by not knowing who I was.

If I sat down in the living room, a footman would appear out of nowhere, plump up the cushions, and erase the indentation I had made. Any impression I made was immediately wiped out. I was unable to find the real me or to feel I had any identity.

When my father died, I asked for one thing only—a china ornament that had been on my mantelpiece in my bedroom ever since I could remember. It was a coach, drawn by horses, with a lady leaning out the window waving a handkerchief. I believe that ornament symbolized to me all the times people had left me behind.

I was a shy child, and never had what it took to be a whiz socially. Furthermore, I was never interested in being one—there were goals that interested me far more.

Many of my friends appear to have thrived on the type of upbringing I had, which was typical of a particular class at a particular time. I certainly didn't thrive. I needed and wanted intimacy with those I loved, but they seemed so far away from me—even physically; I missed coziness and warmth.

A staggering blow to me was my parents' divorce—not so much the divorce as the way it was done. When they were divorced, I was not only devastated by the removal of my father's actual physical presence, but I was also shattered because I was never told anything. I believe I could have understood; I was eleven. I simply heard it from my brother, and I was terribly hurt. We children had been aware of tension—the silent explosive tension hiding under the good breeding. Why had my father not explained to me why he was going away? The next time I heard about him was through the newspapers, which said that he and his new English wife had crashed in a plane on a safari in Africa but were unhurt. How far away he seemed. I loved him, and would have accepted any reason for his leaving. I felt a terrible sense of abandonment and betrayal.

When my father came to visit, he was often distrait; he was there in body but not in spirit. I wanted to hold on to him, to win his admiration, in what seemed like such a short time, and beg him not to leave me alone, that it just hurt to read about him in the papers, going to the races, or playing polo. It all made me feel a million miles away from him, and out of things forever in his life.

I saw him on a visiting basis, but he never was the figure in my life again that I wanted and needed so badly. He loved me when he saw me, but he saw me too rarely, and he was not the best of correspondents.

My mother was obviously very unhappy, living in a world of her own, probably suffering all kinds of problems and miseries, and there seemed no one to turn to or trust. No close aunt or anyone; they were all busy with their own lives.

I became more and more secretive. I buried my feelings and bottled up my emotions.

My father was married for the third time, and we were faced with absorbing two young stepbrothers, and, shortly thereafter, two half-sisters. For a while, I felt jealous and pushed aside, but these relationships have grown into good ones, thanks to a very wise stepmother.

My mother remarried when I was eighteen—in fact, just before I got married. My stepfather was and is a wonderful man, but it was too late for him to feature in my adolescent life.

"So you missed your father very much, didn't you?"

"Yes, most terribly."

Another day: Today we discussed my heredity and

my health record again. Neither one is a subject of great joy.

I said to my doctor, "I knew all my life, even when I was little, that the fact that my father's father committed suicide and that his aunt was not exactly sane preyed on his mind. By a process of osmosis, it began at an early age to prey on mine."

"Why?"

"I don't know–it was sort of catching. And I remember I walked in my sleep while I was growing up, and bars were put on my windows. They made me feel queer because I associated bars on windows with insane people."

"Tell me about your health."

"It was and is lamentable. I don't understand why, because both my parents and my brother and sisters had and have good health. My first memory is one of terror, pain, bright lights, and suffocation, I suppose from an anesthetic–an operation for double mastoid.

"I had every ordinary childhood disease, more than my share of broken bones, plus a concussion which I got from falling off a horse.

"I must have been accident-prone, exceptionally clumsy, or a remarkably bad rider.

"I contracted a series of streptococcus infections, which involved operations and long weeks of hospitalization. There were no antibiotics in those days.

"Apparently I had very little resistance to respiratory infections. Life was one cold on top of the other, interspersed with croup, flu, bronchitis, pneumonia, and other infections.

"Later in life, during the time I was having children and after, I had frequent kidney infections. Then, believe it or not, I had polio, at the age of thirty. Then undulant fever, a stomach ulcer, and a slipped disc, which necessitated weeks spent in traction.

"Polio scared me very much. I came down with it shortly after the birth of my last child. It is truly frightening to feel yourself getting paralyzed all over, and to realize suddenly that you can't move anything. Thank God I could breathe and swallow–I did not have the bulbar type. There were endless sleepless nights when I lay there and just wondered, and didn't dare let myself wonder too long."

"Did it take you a long time to work your way back?"

"Yes, it took me quite a while. I had wonderful care. During the acute phase of the illness I had a Sister Kenny-trained nurse, and later I had an expert therapist. Day after day, we worked, first in a tub filled with swirling water, then on the floor. It was the strangest feeling to have to rack your brain to figure out where your toe was, so you could learn to move it again. My progress was remarkable–first a wheel chair, then crutches, then a cane. Today I can do everything that I was able to do before I had polio. Of course, I get tired more easily, because certain muscles were permanently affected, and I am using others to compensate for them, and I ache a lot from muscle fatigue. But think how lucky I was. I have had, since I can remember, countless allergies. Some are just nuisances, but others involve frightening reactions, such as swelling up all over, and my throat closing off. You might know that among these allergies there would inevitably be numerous drugs, so what cures many a patient overnight, I can't take. Not for me the painless dentist chair, the euphoric dreams induced by morphine, and the miracle penicillin cure. We have to do it the slow, roundabout way.

"I think another reason that made me feel that I was a lonely child was that frequent and repeated illness made me withdraw. I lived in a world of fantasy. If life wasn't pleasant, I was going to make it pleasant. I was out of touch with reality, and I felt isolated and out of things. I had an imaginary companion called Fidelia, to whom I talked constantly.

"Obviously, all these illnesses made me afraid, anxious, and insecure. They produced feelings of discouragement and failure; a constant interruption in school work—in everything. I felt left behind and eventually left out. I was very tense and fearful, which in turn may have led to more illness. It was a vicious circle, and which came first, the chicken or the egg?

"I guess that when a pattern of illness becomes established in a child's life, it results in making that child withdrawn and introspective. It makes him feel out of touch with reality and encourages any tendency to escape into the realm of fantasy.

"I was a conscientious child, eager to meet the high standards expected of me, and each illness was a slap in the face. Life became stretches of living between illnesses.

"There was a lack of continuity in my life and the sense of accomplishment that comes from finishing things. I would lose parts in plays in school and was considered undependable. I developed a feeling that there was not time to do things; hence I had to do them right away, right then in a hurry, and nothing could wait. To be truthful, I still feel there will never be time enough to do the things I must; hence my compulsive drive to get them done without any delay.

"Each time I was sick it became harder and harder to get back in the mainstream and I felt different, queer, apart, and isolated. I had a sense of shame and guilt.

"I wish now that at these times I had had some psychiatric help because I bottled up all these emotions and fears and stresses.

"I'll say one thing, though–I emerged from this morass of ailments with a great many inner resources, plus one hell of a resolve not to waste one single second of health. Unfortunately this resolve can produce an overenthusiasm to make up for lost time, so that I tackle far too much all at once. Consequently I get overtired, run down, and thereby lay myself wide open for some other lurking bug that is waiting to set up residence in this object I call my body, and which I wish I could have turned in on a new model long ago. I don't see how you can win, really.

"Out of this tale of medical woe has come a tremendous sense of shame on my part about being sick. Therefore I want to hide not only the ailment, but myself as well. I will run around with a temperature of 103 rather than admit that I am ill *again*.

"I am ashamed when I come into a hospital and have to give my medical history to some eager intern. I get the feeling that he must be thinking that the specimen lying at his midwaist will disintegrate if he attempts to test its reflexes and that he will think that I am exaggerating my illnesses."

When my doctor came today, he said, "Tell me about your loneliness as a child."

"I lived in big houses on a floor away from my parents, with my governess. I rarely saw my sister, who was much younger than I, and my brother was sent away to boarding school at a very young age."

"What did you do to help your loneliness?" my doctor asked.

"I told you, I made up an imaginary companion," I said. "Her name was Fidelia. I used to talk to her, read to her, play the piano with her, and share games of jacks and hopscotch. We spent many many hours together."

"How long did you keep this imaginary companion?"

"I don't remember the exact time at which she faded away. I got married when I was very young, and I had four children. Believe me, you don't need any one imaginary to talk to with four children around. But I'll tell you one thing–delusional or not, I conjured up Fidelia's ghost during those endless lonely days when I was locked in my room at that other hospital. I know it's considered a touch daft to talk to yourself, but since I was in a mental hospital for being emotionally ill, I thought I might as well make the most of it."

"Was she any help to you?"

"Not much. She remained a child, and I have grown up, and besides, she stopped answering me anymore. When I was a child, she used to answer me."

"You and I are going to do a lot of talking, and I don't think you will need her anymore. We are going to exorcise her ghost along with a lot of others. Tell me, did you have any depressions, other than postnatal ones, during your life before you got this acute one?"

"Yes, when I had undulant fever. That's a depressing, extremely painful, and seemingly endless disease—there is no treatment—it just has to burn itself out. I don't understand why I got depressed after each child was born. I was so thrilled and excited to have the baby, then I would get these inexplicable depressions."

"This is something we don't know too much about, you know. New drugs are helping in these cases, though, which certainly shows some relationship to the chemicophysical makeup of a person. And I know that drugs are going to help you now."

"I hope so."

Another day: My doctor asked me today what I thought the recent and current pressures, tensions, anxieties, and fears have been and were in my life. So I told him that within a relatively short span of time, several things happened that were a strain to me.

My sister married a Negro. I was shocked at first, but what upset me most was the schism that took place in the family at that time, and her complete rejection by some of the family—the severance of all ties and relationships. I have come not only to accept the idea, which I admit was strange and foreign at first, and certainly unexpected, but to love my sister's husband and their children, although it was difficult at first to accept them as part of me. I think today we have a closer bond than ever, that our relationship is even more loving, for which I thank God in this much split family. I cannot see that love for a child or a brother or sister has to change because you do not entirely understand him or her.

Then in 1956 I was on the *Andrea Doria*, with two of my children, when she was rammed by the *Stockholm*, and sank. This was a terrifying ordeal, a night of horror and terror that I think I shall never forget.

Very shortly after this, my father started dying of brain cancer. This slow dying, watching him die with his little night cap on his poor shaven head, sitting in his room holding his hand, waiting for him to sometimes know me and sometimes not, tore me apart emotionally more than I can say. For his sake, I could not break down in front of him. We played records sometimes, whose melodies still pull at my heartstrings when I hear them today.

We watched him literally melt away, and the night he died, something infinitely precious and irreplaceable, of which I had had not nearly enough, went out of my life, finally and forever. Even in his death, and I am a big girl, I thought he had abandoned me again.

Just before my father's death, my brother had a mental illness that rocked my emotional boat almost to the point of tipping it over. I was witness for the first time to what can happen to a mind, one of the finest minds I know, when it breaks and becomes so emotionally upset that it goes beyond the bounds of rationality. He became completely well, but how was I to know that at the time of his illness?

I will never forget my brother at my father's funeral. He came, under heavy sedation, and I think he was unaware of what was going on, living in another world.

He and I had been unusually close through the years. I was conscious of him behind me all through the funeral, and I was afraid of what he would do or say. I felt more abandoned and alone than ever, because he too was beyond my reach and could not share my feelings as we had shared so many things in our lives.

His illness shocked me profoundly, and I suppose I tended to identify with him a certain amount.

I became frighteningly familiar with the locked hospital in which he was a patient, and in spite of the plush red carpets, horrified about some of the, to me, astonishing rules and prohibitions, good and bad floors, and "shock treatment," that dreaded word. I did not like what I saw; it haunted me and I was afraid.

My visits to him upset me beyond words. I could not reach him, really; he was at that time a changed human being and a stranger—that is what affected me the most.

Each time I left, he would beg me to take him with me, and I had to hear that door clang between him and me. I would go down to the lobby and cry my heart out. I think part of me stayed behind that locked door with him. Furthermore, I had the feeling that somehow I was going to be next.

5

Talks and Treatment

"Why do you think you always wanted to succeed so much, and what did you have in mind as 'being a success'?"

"That is a hard question to answer. I think I really wanted to succeed for my parents' sake. It wasn't for me; I don't think I cared. It was for them."

"And did you succeed?"

"I never felt I did. As I have become older, I have ceased to strive desperately to become the famous figure I thought in my childhood that I had to become. Instead I have come to believe that the most important thing is to succeed in your relationships with other people. This comes way ahead of any 'fame' the like of which I dreamed of obtaining so long ago. You know, that's the reason that the final admission to myself that my marriage is a failure is one of the hardest things I have ever had to accept, because it is a failure in a human relationship, and you may be hurting not only you and your husband, but your children. I vowed I would never hurt my children this way, because I missed my father so much after my parents were divorced, and I felt abandoned."

"And you blame yourself entirely for this failure?"

"Yes."

"Has it ever occurred to you that part of the failure could be laid on the shoulders of the man you married?"

"No, it hasn't, not in my deepest heart."

"Well, I must make you see that at least some of the failure is not yours. I think you are reaching an understanding of some of the motives for which you married, which were wrong motives."

"That is scant comfort when you have to pick up so many pieces of your shattered hopes and dreams. But you know, yesterday I was thinking of the continual feeling I always had, and still have, of being abandoned. I could never let go of a man even if I knew really and truly that he was not the right man for me, because his going out of my life would have meant being abandoned again, and I could not face that."

"Even though it was you this time who might be doing the abandoning?"

"I never thought of it that way. Yes, even though it might have been I who was doing it, it would have felt as if I were the one being abandoned."

"Why do you think you have such a sense of abandonment? Tell me more about it."

"I wish I understood it better. I even feel abandoned when my husband goes to work in the morning, or when one of my children goes away to school, or even when visitors leave after a weekend. It is a feeling that frightens me beyond words and makes me unhealthily and abnormally overdependent on my husband and certain other people. Even now, when I know I must get out of my marriage, I still feel a sense of abandonment."

"Yet you are the one who feels the overwhelming necessity for this divorce."

"Yes, I do. After eighteen years of trying to make our marriage work, I can see that there is no other way to go on living, and yet I am going to feel abandoned and alone when it comes to pass, even though I know that it must be done–in fact, I now think it should have been done sooner. It's the years of tearing doubt that finally bring you to the breaking point; hanging on because of the children and the fear of being alone and abandoned, even though, as you say, it is I who wants to get out of this marriage. I know that a better relationship in a marriage must exist than there is and has been for many years in ours. Do you think unconsciously I have been getting even for my feelings of abandonment as a child by wanting a divorce?"

"No, I don't. From what you tell me, you both tried to keep this marriage going for eighteen years. You, for one, sought help to do so. As for your apparent contradictory thought that you will feel abandoned, when you are the one who wants to get out of the marriage, I don't find it so contradictory. It is really an unrealistic fear carried to an extreme. I believe that once you have actually gone through the divorce, you will be able to stand alone. You and I have discussed the problem of your marriage, and you have decided that to get a divorce is the only possible thing for you to do if you are going to get well and stay well."

"I know, I know, but it is awfully hard to face the fact that I have failed—failed my children, failed my husband; and never for a moment have we fooled the children. They have sensed the tension and undercurrents of misery. We tried to wait for a divorce until they were old enough to understand, but I failed, I never fooled them."

"Now, wait a minute. Try not to see all the failure as yours. I think you have tried pretty hard to make the marriage work."

"But don't you see that I have failed?"

"All right, you have failed. We all fail sometimes. It doesn't fit in with your obsession with perfection, does it?"

"No, it doesn't."

"Why do you think you keep making demands on yourself to be perfect all the time?"

"Because I wanted so badly to be perfect when I was a child, and I missed the goal by so much."

"Do you think that you could stop thinking as a child now, and realize that none of us reaches the goal of perfection we may have set for ourselves, and yet we are not failures because of it?"

"I will try to think of that—try to stop being a child."

"It's always 'I' that failed, isn't it? No chance of 'we'? I think many of us have failed and made good later. Don't you see that some of us have to fail in order to succeed? There are very seldom successes without some failures along the way, or if there are, it is for the exceptionally fortunate of this world. If people did not have the courage to try different things, there would be no failures, granted, but neither would there be any successes."

"I can't look at it like that. You see, I haven't had a career. I have just had marriage and children."

"You can call that a career, and I think in your mind you do. You have compared marriage to my career or careers."

"Yes, but in the failure of a marriage there are so many pieces to pick up, and so many people are involved—not just you."

"That could happen in a career too. If a man fails at his job, his family feels it."

"You just said 'failed'."

"Yes, I did, and you see the word 'failed' is not that terrible to face. If a man fails at his job, he will try to get another, and succeed at that one."

"You can't go on looking at marriage that way, with children involved."

"You can't go on failing indefinitely in a marriage, but you can allow yourself some degree of failure without feeling that your life as a whole has been a failure. You must take your life as a whole."

"I will try. Right now I don't see any successes anywhere."

"You will. You will come to see that this pattern of perfection you established in your childhood mind is not really reasonable."

"Did I make that pattern, or did others?"

"Both, I think. Someone established the pattern, and you continued it. Do you resent not having seen more of your parents, particularly your father?"

"No, 'resent' is not really the word. Perhaps I resented it when I was little, and for a while I thought that was the way everyone saw their parents, until I was older and saw differently. Then it made me more sad than anything else. I think we, and they, missed something very precious and irreplaceable. It takes day-to-day closeness and intimacy to build up a good relationship between children and parents. I have tried to do it with mine. Right now I'm failing."

"You had to be a perfect parent, didn't you?"

"I would have liked to have been one."

"Well, I think you have been a pretty good one."

Another day: "Tell me why you think God has turned his back on you."

"It is hard to put into words. When I was little, I had an image of God up in the sky, and he was a very stern man with a beard, and for some reason he looked like a gardener–he had a big hoe in his hand. I always thought of Christ as being gentler and more forgiving. I don't feel He has turned His back on me so much, and sometimes I can pray to Him. I have never been able to put God and Christ together in my mind."

"What was your religious upbringing?"

"Confusing, I think. We were baptized Catholics, but we were not brought up in the Catholic church. One parent was Catholic, and one was Presbyterian, but neither went to church much that I can remember, except on Christmas or Easter. I went to the Catholic church when I was little, when I had a Catholic governess. Then I went to the Protestant church when I had a Protestant governess, or I did not go to any church. In school I started to go to the Episcopal church, because that is where most of my friends went, and I was confirmed in the Episcopal church. The odd thing is that when I am in trouble, like, for instance, when my son was so sick when he was a baby, I went to find a Catholic church near the hospital, to pray and burn a candle. I think I did this because a Catholic church is always open, and I turned to it in the same way I did as a small child, when I most needed to pray; some leftover part of my childhood must have derived comfort from burning a candle in front of Christ and His mother or a saint. It gave me a very personal and intimate feeling. But, you see, there is no possibility of my turning to any church now, because I have broken the rules to get a divorce. This does not mean that I don't have any faith anymore; it is just that now it is a private belief, and not one that I can express through any particular church or faith. I am almost sure that Christ has not turned his back on me. As a child I had a wonderful picture of Him in my room, and I have never forgotten the look in his eyes of compassion and understanding; but I formed a strange image of God–I suppose because there was nothing specific to look at. You know, it is amazing what a lot of strange fears and superstitions you are exposed to as a child if you spend a lot of time with nurses and governesses. They had theories on everything, from how to cure warts to the sex life of pigeons in the park. A child is gullible–at least, I was–and although I thought a lot of these theories were full of bunk, nevertheless I was not sure, and they filled me full of doubts, and sometimes fears."

"Why didn't you discuss them with your parents?"

"Maybe they were not around at the time I wanted to, and a child forgets—in his conscious mind, anyway—and a lot of odd things get filed away behind that conscious mind. Anyway, I kept a lot of things to myself, and mulled them over for hours. I probably came up with some silly conclusions."

Another day: "You say that as a child you lived a lot in a world of fantasy. Why?"

"I guess because I like it there. I had a first cousin just my age; we were as close as sisters. We spent many summers together. We were both full of fantasies and shared a marvelous secret life. When we were quite young we would sneak out of bed around five-thirty every summer morning in the country to explore a wonder world, part real, part fantasy, in our bare feet and nightgowns. We got away with this for a long time, because we returned to our beds before anyone else was awake. One day, to our horror, we ran right into my governess on the stairs, who was furious because, I suppose, she had worried about our beds being empty and because our feet were wet. Sometimes I wonder if we were not overprotected, you know. After all, there is really no harm in exploring at five-thirty in the morning. Some children are neglected, and some are overprotected. I think there must be a happy medium somewhere. Anyway, that was the end of our secret, magic world for a while, but we were pretty good at building other ones wherever we went together. We practically lived in each other's fantasies; it was rather an extraordinary and unique relationship for many years, and a wonderful one. You see, my sister was five years younger than I, and I didn't see much of her during those years. When I was alone, I told myself stories—endless stories in serial form that I would drag on for weeks."

"Where did the ideas for the stories come from?"

"Oh, out of my mind and books—especially books like *The Swiss Family Robinson.* We were children who spent considerable time alone. I think that was a good thing in many ways, because we developed inner resources, which you do when you are fairly isolated; yet it had its disadvantages too. When I was older, I felt ill at ease and 'out of it' when some of my friends seemed so at ease in what amounted to a group or a clique—they were part of something that I could never feel a part of. Now that I look back on it, I don't think it affected my life one way or another. I still am not much of a 'joiner,' and who is to say whether that is good or bad, desirable or undesirable?"

"I agree, except that you should be able to take it or leave it, and it is all right to leave it because you do not want to join, but not because you feel ill at ease if you do."

Another day: "Why do you think I have this obsession about the quotation from the poem *The Hound of Heaven* about fleeing, and footsteps following me? Sometimes it is all I can think about, like a tune you try to get out of your head and cannot, no matter how hard you try.

> "I fled Him, down the nights and down the days;
> I fled Him, down the arches of the years;
> I fled Him, down the labyrinthine ways
> Of my own mind; and in the mist of tears
> I hid from Him, and under running laughter.
> Up vistaed hopes I sped;
> And shot, precipitated,
> Adown Titanic glooms of chasméd fears,
> From those strong Feet that followed, followed after."

"Many things become obsessive when you are in the state you are in, but we'll have to find out why this particular obsession sticks so thoroughly in your mind that at times it excludes all other thoughts."

"Could I be that guilty?"

"No, but in your estimation you seem to be. You appear to have a very powerful sense of guilt, which must have started when you were a small child."

Another day: One of my closest friends, a priest, flew on from Chicago to see me. I need him—he knows me and my family so well.

He was allowed to take me to a bench that overlooks the river. It was a warm and sunny day. I felt so weak and uncoordinated—my legs reacted like cooked noddles. I had, also, a terrible sinking feeling of dread. It must be like the dread a man has before he goes into battle.

We sat on the bench for a long time and watched the day excursion boats. They looked so free. I couldn't go on one of them then. I was still a prisoner, trapped in my own mind. It stood out so clearly.

We were together, my friend and I, yet I was alone. It was that glass wall, that invisible glass wall between us. Even he was slipping farther and farther away and getting dimmer. I thought, "I still see you, my friend, but I cannot touch you anymore. I am a sick Alice through the looking glass. I try to touch your hand, but you are not really there to touch. I feel as if I am looking at you through a kaleidoscope; you are all broken up into little fragments, and you never stay the same for more than a second."

I said to him, "I have turned against myself. Why has God turned His face away from me too?"

He answered, "Any suffering has to be offered up to God, to be laid at His feet. Someday you will be the wiser for all this pain now. He hasn't turned his back on you."

"Wiser," I exclaimed. "I'm crazy."

"Not now, but someday," he explained.

I said, "Someday—how do you know there will be a someday? I must have done something awful to deserve this."

"Your present agony has absolutely nothing to do with what you have done or left undone. God has reasons beyond our understanding."

"But it isn't just God who is beyond understanding. I feel abandoned, not only by Him, but by everyone. Oh, please save me."

He said quietly, "I am praying for you, and you must pray."

"But don't you see that I can't pray? You see, I know I must get a divorce; there is no other answer for me, and I can't pray for that. I should be praying for the strength to keep our marriage together, but I've been doing that for years. I can't pray to get well so that I can get a divorce–it is against the Episcopal church and most of my religious beliefs; but I know I must get out of this marriage to get well, and stay well."

"You can pray to get well. God will give you His answer eventually."

"But you don't understand," I cried. "His answer won't be the one I can accept. Don't you see, He's left me. I see Him up there–His back is turned on me. You must see, I don't want the marriage to last anymore. I've tried for eighteen years. I won't pray to make the marriage last–I'm through praying for that, because it is a dishonest prayer. But no more, my friend, no more. This is the trap that is making me ill and keeping me ill. It is no good telling yourself that some people stick it out. For the sake of the children, you know we've tried."

"And yet you tell me that you are terrified to have your husband fly down to Florida on business, and at the same time you don't want him around."

"Oh, I know it's awful for him; I am unhealthily dependent on him, disliking him more because of it. Perhaps I am afraid that at the bottom, if something happened to him, I would have wished it on him without being conscious of it. I don't even want to be abandoned by someone I have come to wish was out of my life. I clutch on to anything. Oh, why does a marriage that has gone wrong turn into hate?"

"Because of the weakness of human beings who expect too much; when they don't receive it, they blame each other."

"I don't blame him, I blame myself. You see, my guilt is this: I know divorce is wrong, you know it's wrong, you're a Catholic, but it has to be, even though it may hurt a lot of people, but I think they will be hurt less in the long run this way."

"I know it's against my church, but you still feel I care about you, don't you?"

"Yes."

"That's all that matters now. If I love you, you know God must love you."

"No, I don't. The sun has gone into the river. Please take me back to my hospital room, but just stay for a little while."

Back in my room, I said, "I can't even begin to get my tortured feelings across to you; I can't get them into words. There are no words you or anyone can understand."

"You wrote it better in a letter. I think you can communicate better that way. I came because I wanted to comfort you as much as I could. Keep writing to me."

"My speech is dammed up. Oh, God, someone must listen, even though I am inarticulate, and understand and stay close to me and accept me still."

"I do, God does, many people do. Have faith, little one, have faith. You have a doctor you can talk to now."

"No, I have no faith. I promised to knit you a pair of cable-stitch socks, and I can't even do that."

"You will, and I'll hold you to it."

He left, and I felt as if one of my last anchors to sanity went with him, not because he is a priest (I have no faith just now), but because I need him.

Another day: Someone in my family is trying to get me back into a closed place. Whoever it is said I was making no progress here. What do they expect, a miracle? I am making progress. I should know. Why do I have to be in a closed place? I have not made one iota of trouble here, and I have done everything I've been told to do.

The floor nurse found me crying and asked me what was the matter. I told her that I was terrified about being sent back to a closed place, and she sent for my doctor. He came, thank God, and he comforted me, and told me that no one could take me away from where I was or from him, so long as I wanted to stay.

Another day: Where anger and fear have been, there is now love. My doctor trusts me, and I trust him. This trust is stronger than the desire to kill myself, and overcomes fear. He said someday I will get better. I have to reach more inward in order to be able to rid myself of all the things that made me ill. Then I shall feel more peaceful and comfortable in my mind again, and this wretched brain of mine will stop turning in circles. I shall be able to live with it again. I can't live with it now; it is too painful, and yet I am still trapped in it.

I say to my doctor, "If I were very sick–for instance, if I had cancer–I would still be myself. The way I am sick now, I am not myself. How are we going to find the self that was me?"

"We will find it, and you will perhaps find a stronger and better self. I can feel how much you are suffering now, and it is hard for you to believe what I say. If you had cancer, you might be yourself for a while, but you might never get well, either; in fact, you might die."

"How can you feel the suffering? You have never been crazy."

"You are not crazy; you must get this straight. You frighten yourself by using this word."

"But they said at the other hospital that I had crossed the line, and I must say I had to agree."

"Well, forget that, and don't misinterpret it as meaning that you are crazy or insane. As for feeling your suffering, I have seen enough of it to be able to feel it."

"When will I get well? When? In a day, a week, a month, a year, five years?"

"I cannot tell you exactly."

"I don't know, today, that you are real. I am so alone, and you seem so far away."

"I am real," he said, touching me.

"You would not lie to me about getting well, would you?"

"No, I would never lie to you."

After he left, I thought, "He has become everything to me. He has promised me that I will get well. He is real; he will help me and save me. I feel the leading hand of gentleness and caring. No one else exists just now."

Another day: My doctor asked me today, "What

do you think a nervous breakdown is? It is a rather meaningless term except to the layman, you know."

"Well, I would say you came apart at the seams. Your brain has no fences left with which to enclose your imagination and fantasies. Your innermost mind feels bare, and all out in the open. Sometimes you can hardly breathe, and you can't tell anyone why, because you cannot find the words and you are trying too hard to go on breathing. I don't think it is your nerves, exactly, although they feel like violin strings that have snapped. I think it is your mind that breaks, sort of in two, as if it had a crack down the middle."

"Is that the way it feels?"

"Yes."

"I must explain to you, though, about your form of mental illness, so that you do not think that you are insane, and so that you will believe and know that there will be an end to your illness, and that your mind will be as good as it ever was, and as whole."

"But it is hard to understand this thing that is happening to me. Why can't I just wake up one morning and be well again, and feel that the crack in my mind is healed? It cracked overnight, so why can't it heal overnight?"

"I don't think it really cracked overnight, although it may have felt like that to you; and if it did, a bone that is cracked in a minute does not heal overnight. It will take time and work, patience and faith, to make your mind whole again."

"Someday will it all appear like a bad dream?"

"Someday it will."

"I have always known about being depressed, but this is different. This is not a depression, you see; this is an entirely strange, dark world I am living in. I have lost my mind."

"You have not lost it, or you would not have looked for help in order to get better. You are very much aware of a great many realities. You must understand this. Your mind is sick, but you have not lost it—it just seems to you as if you had. I told you we will make your mind well, you and I."

"How? You don't know me that well, really."

"But I shall know you better and better. We will take it step by step together. I see you want to give, to talk; that is a good start."

"Am I going to need shock treatment?"

"You asked me that before. I can only say that you might need it if all drugs fail and if you do not keep showing improvement, and your suffering does not get less."

"Don't leave me. My mind and my sanity depend on you."

"I have to. I will be back tomorrow. Will you do me a favor? Stop referring to yourself as a nut or insane, and stop talking about nut houses?"

"All right. I'll refer to myself as mentally disturbed, and the nut—I mean hospital as a mental institution."

Another day: I had a note from one of the children today: just "Dear Mummie, I love you." It made me cry.

Another day*: One day I found myself struggling with all my strength to get out of a dream, a dream that kept pulling me back and back into it, and would not let me go. The dream was made up of flashes of Peter-Pan-like scenes. I was Wendy, only I was doomed to fly perpetually over an endless Never-Never Land, and I was Pinocchio at the time he began to turn into a donkey, and his ears grew bigger and bigger because he had been bad. There were people all around me, in a house with so many doors through which they kept entering and leaving that I could never catch up with one of them long enough to find a familiar face. I cried out again and again, "I know you, I know you, please show me your faces." I tried to catch hold of them, but they were always just out of reach. It was as if I had almost drowned, but if I could hold my breath just a little longer I would reach the surface. It seemed that I struggled forever. I was trying to recapture the dream, and yet to get out of it.

Then all at once I was walking through a garden. Flowers were blooming, and I reached down to pick one. By my side was a woman with gray hair and a white uniform. We walked across a street to a river, where I smelled the sea and saw boats floating by on the sparkling water. I did not wonder who the woman was

*I have no recollection of the exact time during my stay in the hospital at which I received shock treatments. Evidently I continued to function somehow, but I remember nothing of the time just before the treatments or during them, with the exception of the last three or four treatments. I have placed this period of time in the continuity of my story as accurately as I have been able to.

who walked with me, or how I came to be where I was. I just smelled the river-sea smell, the flowers I had picked, and the grass. The air touched me with tenderness. I watched a sea gull glide over the river, and its cry reached me, standing on the shore. I was overcome by a poignant nostalgia.

As my companion and I walked once more through the garden, I saw that there was a wall around it. I looked up, up, beyond the height of the wall, and I saw a tall building that appeared to touch the clouds.

"Where am I?" I asked my companion.

"We are taking a walk outside of the hospital, dear," she answered. "Isn't it a lovely day?"

"Yes," I said, "it is the most beautiful day of all. I can see, I can smell, I can hear, I can touch, and I know it is springtime. This wall I see does not close me in, does it? I am back in the real world, aren't I?"

"Yes, dear," she answered, smiling at me, "you are back in the real world."

"Shall I be able to stay in it?" I asked.

"Yes, you will be able to stay in it almost all of the time now. How does it feel to be back in the real world?"

"Oh, Lord," I thought, "there is no answer I can give to this kind woman to express my feelings, but thank you, Lord, please let me stay."

Another day: I must have gone through another blank period. When I woke up today I was in a room that looked familiar, yet strange. I thought for a long time, and the room grew less strange. I recognized it as my room in the hospital. I felt that there was no place for fear, that I was standing on a pinnacle where there was nothing but light. If there were problems, they could all be solved. I felt I understood everything, more than ever before; I was intoxicated—drunk with happiness. I wanted to share my feelings with my doctor, right then. When he came into my room, I hugged him, and he smiled and said, "There's a lot of warmth there, isn't there? What a wonderful thing it is to see you smile."

I said, "Who do you go to when you are depressed and afraid? Do you have someone like you to make you feel all whole again? Why do I feel like this?"

"I have been giving you shock treatments."

"But I thought you were not going to."

"I know, but you were getting no better; in fact, you were getting worse, and I could not bear to see you suffer so. Don't you remember signing for the treatments?"

"Signing for them! I don't remember anything for ages. I never would have signed for them in my right mind. But I guess I wasn't in my right mind, was I?"

"Do you resent the fact that I gave you shock treatments, or feel I betrayed you?"

"How could I resent anything or feel betrayed when I feel like this? Have I just had a treatment?"

"Yes. I must tell you, you won't feel like this all the time. You are not yet coping with any problems or facing life outside this room."

"I know, but I shall be able to cope with anything now."

"You have improved a great deal, and you will

improve more. I am going to give you more treatments."

"How do you do the treatments so I don't know about them?"

"Now that your memory has returned in part, you will be aware that you are going to have treatments. But you will not mind. I give you sodium Pentothal, and you go to sleep before you can count to three. I am happy to see you better, and I will see you tomorrow."

After he left, my wonderful mirage began to fade. I had a terrible, almost unbearable headache. But I hugged some of the mirage close to me. I could not let it all get away from me. I had to hang on to a remnant of it. "I hope I regain my memory," I thought.

Another day: This morning I was playing canasta with a nurse, when my doctor came into my room and asked me, "Do you remember your daughter coming to see you, and leaving a request for you to have your hair cut?"

"No; did I have a haircut?"

"Look at yourself in the mirror."

I was a little afraid to look, but I looked. I think I recognized myself a little.

"How do you think you look?"

"I look more like me; don't you think so?"

"I don't know what you looked like before you came here, but you look better than I have ever seen you look."

"My eyes don't look so vacant. I used to look in a mirror, and nothing seemed to be reflected in it. Now I see me. I look pale, but it is me."

"Tomorrow I shall give you another shock treatment."

I felt as if a huge black cloud had suddenly passed over my warm, comforting, sun-drenched world.

"I am afraid," I said.

"Don't be; nothing will hurt or bother you—just a bad headache afterward."

I think the nurses knew that I was afraid. That evening a nice young English resident spent almost an hour with me, helping me with my jigsaw puzzle and telling me about his life in England. He should be a wonderful doctor, because he makes one feel as if he really cares. I didn't tell him I was afraid, but I know he knew it, and he tried so hard to make me less afraid.

My nightmare terrors are somewhat numb, but still I know I must always be on guard. If I lose my footing and I plunge once again to the bottom of the abyss, will I once more be able to pull myself all the way up that endless and at times seemingly hopeless incline? I grow weary at times of keeping my foot from slipping even a little. Daylight disappeared for me before, and I know it can do so again. My mind was lost to me before, and I know it can be lost to me again.

I grow weary of clinging to the flimsy and frail rope bridge that sways with the winds of my still-uncontrollable mind, over a chasm without bottom; weary of sitting on the lid of a box that forever stands in a dark corner, so that it will stay locked, with not a chink through which these formless, nameless, reasonless terrors can worm their way out.

I feel, not always, but sometimes, like the particularly harassed "old lady who lived in a shoe and had so many children she didn't know what to do." I am tired of retrieving thoughts that are trying to get away from me, grabbing one by the heel, one by the scruff of the neck, another by the seat of the pants—I haven't enough hands. I grow weary of keeping the vise tight that keeps the separation small and close between what my intelligence and intellect tell me, and what I feel, which is far less controllable. The extent to which this vise stays closed is an indication of the growth I have made from mental illness back to the realm of normalcy.

I grow weary of steering clear of the lamp that needs only to be brushed against to release all those evil genies.

How long shall I be haunted like this? Forever? My brain and intellect tell me that the same set of circumstances which brought me to my illness no longer exists, but when will I really know it, and believe it in my heart and soul, and above all, when will I feel it?

I must have faith. Although I may slip back down periodically, the next peak will be higher, and finally I will reach the highest one of all, where all the world will be spread out at my feet, without mist, clear and shimmering in the light as far as the eye can see.

Another day: When my doctor came today I told him, "The bars around me now are of my own making, aren't they?"

"Soon we will remove them," he said.

Another day: Today was a banner day.

Around noon a friend of mine brought me an angel cake with white icing—he knows it is my favorite kind of cake. I wondered, as I tried to make polite conversation, if he had the remotest conception of my disturbed feelings. But I was touched because he still thought of me as a human being, with one of my senses, at least, unchanged, even though he knew I was having a "nervous breakdown."

Toward evening, another friend came to visit me. A few years ago, he had the same type of illness as mine. His presence in my room was a comfort. I knew, without any words being spoken, that he understood what I was going through. Even this slight contact, this glimpse of a feeling of being close to someone, was a help to me. I felt like begging him to stay when it came time for him to leave. He promised to come back, and I know he will.

Another day: "You sleep with less medication now, don't you?"

"Oh, yes. I go to sleep with the television still going, quite early, and I am beginning to sleep as if I had never slept before."

"Do you still have any delusions? For instance, does the furniture threaten you like you said the bureau did at home?"

"No, not really. That bureau at the end of my bed here got a little threatening the other day, but I got up and smacked it, and told it that it was nothing but a bureau, and it hasn't bothered me since."

"Do you still think someone is following you?"

"I don't go anyplace, so if someone is following me, he or it has no place to follow."

Another day: When my doctor came today, I said, "Look what I have made during these past days. You see, I can make it into a tabletop. You stick all these mosaics together in a pattern or design that you like."

"Do you enjoy doing it?"

"Yes, I do."

"I've been pleased to see you keep busy this way, because there is no planned program of activity here. The nurses tell me that you knit, do needlework, paint a bit. This is good. What do you think motivates you to do these things?"

"I don't know. I like to be creative, I think. Also I like to make things for other people that I think will surprise or please them, or because it will make our house nicer, or one of my children look nice if I make him or her something like a sweater. You know, I do these things when I am well too, although there is much less time to do them then. It brings me a sense of satisfaction and accomplishment."

"How did you do in school?"

"O.K., with ups and downs. I ended up president of the school."

"Was it expected of you to do well?"

"Oh, yes, and I wanted to be perfect. I had a few rebellions on the way up, though."

Another day: I look forward to my doctor's visits because I feel each time, after he has left, that I have rid myself of a huge burden. Sometimes I stand at my window and watch for him to come out of the building across the street where he has his office. I also watch the construction of a second layer on the George Washington Bridge. I wonder if I will ever get to use it.

Another day: "Tell me a little about how you feel about boats. You told me that you were on the *Andrea Doria* when she was rammed and sunk by the *Stockholm.* Did you panic then?"

"You know, I have often thought about panic in the sense that I felt it on that ship. There were bad moments during that night of horror."

"Tell me about it."

"We had two of our children with us; Barbara, sixteen at the time, and Bobby, who was twelve.

"The most shocking thing was the collision. In this day and age, with radar, you don't expect to run into another ship. My husband and I were playing bridge at the time of the collision. We were thrown from our seats. I got in a terrible panic trying to reach our son's cabin, two decks below the place we had been playing bridge. For a while it looked as if we were not going to be able to reach him—the passageway was blocked with debris and sloshing water, and there was so much steam I couldn't see, I thought it was smoke, and became even more frightened. I had long since taken off my shoes; the passageways were covered with oil, and very slippery. We did manage to reach Bobby's cabin, which, thank God, was still there; starting three cabins away from his, there were no cabins left—they had been sheared away by the ice-cutting prow of the *Stockholm.*

"My son had been thrown out of bed onto the floor, but he was still asleep. We awakened him, grabbed our life preservers, and rushed frantically to find our daughter. She had been dancing in the lounge when last seen. Thank heaven, she had the sense to go to our lifeboat station, figuring we would probably bring her life preserver. Take my advice and always go to a boat drill—we went, with lots of laughs, but I'm glad we went.

"I guess the toughest part was the endless wait, lying flat on the tilting promenade deck, trying not to kick the heads of the people stacked up at your feet, waiting to hear something over the loudspeaker system, and hearing nothing except the crew talking to each other in Italian, not knowing if help was on the way, and feeling the ship listing more and more every minute. Now and then the *Doria* blew long blasts. I heard a woman scream, and then a slap followed.

"I was aware of two priests carrying a cup around, which I assumed was the last communion. One of the priests, the younger one, who had been in the navy during the war, told us how to handle ourselves in case we had to jump into the water—to jump with one hand holding one's nose, on account of the oil in the water, and the other hand pulling down one's life jacket, so at impact it would not break one's neck.

"I looked over the edge of the deck and couldn't conceive of jumping from where we were—it was about three stories high. We decided that my husband would hang on to Bobby, and Barbara and I would hang on to each other, if we had to go in the ocean. I was afraid the water would be cold—cold water takes my breath away. My mouth was so dry, I could barely breathe already.

"Finally a steward came and said that women and children were to follow him, but he didn't say where we were going. There ensued a scene in which my son refused to leave his father, until the steward, who knew us, said to him, 'Bobby, you must take care of your mother and your sister,' and changed his mind for him.

"Sliding down crazily tilted decks was nothing compared to that horrible period of waiting, and not knowing what was going to happen. I slid up against a rail somewhere, looked up, and saw enormous bright lights, the *Ile de France*. God, what a sight that was. When our turn came, we slid down ropes into a lifeboat. The old people were pathetic; they would panic halfway down a rope ladder and be unable to go either up or down. Some people were jumping into the water and swimming to the lifeboats. There was a moment when I thought our lifeboat was going to tip over–it was dangerously overloaded, and the crew had difficulty pulling away from the *Doria*. I was torn between pity for those in the water and self-preservation.

"I was proud of our children in the lifeboat. Barbara was trying to help a woman with a badly cut head, and Bobby, who was scrunched up on my lap, yelled, 'Well, at least we don't have to go through customs,' a comment which made everyone laugh.

"I was afraid of climbing up the ladder on the *Ile de France*–it looked awfully long and high, and although the sea was comparatively calm, there was quite a swell that involved a bit of expert timing. The sailors on the lifeboat tied a rope around Bobby, to his utter disgust. Of all of us, he was probably the last one who would have fallen between the lifeboat and the *Ile de France*.

"When I stepped aboard the *Ile de France*, a sailor kissed me on both cheeks and said, '*Eh bien, Madame, c'est fini, n'est-ce-pas, et tout va bien.*' I said nothing—I was afraid I would break down and cry.

"We were led to deck chairs on the promenade deck and plied with coffee, cigarettes, whiskey, and even shoes. Just as I was beginning to get worried, my husband showed up, having arrived in an almost empty lifeboat.

"When the *Ile* finally pulled out, mission accomplished, and headed back toward New York, I was standing next to a French sailor. We watched the *Doria*, with her three swimming pools showing, just starting to go down. The sailor was weeping. It didn't seem possible that that beautiful ship, known proudly in Italy as the Queen of Ships, could disappear forever, with only God knew how many dead aboard.

"I'll never forget the *Ile de France*'s reception in the harbor of New York. People lined the shores for miles; every boat blew her whistle and raised and lowered her flags. Helicopters hovered overhead taking pictures. I was leaning against the rail of the promenade deck with Bobby, and for the first time I cried. Bobby, still clad in his oil-stained pajamas, said, 'What is there to cry about now, for heaven's sake?' "

"You do hold your emotions inside you quite a bit," commented my doctor. "You'd be better off if you could let them off at the time you feel them."

"I know I would be. I envy people who don't feel they have to hold back their tears—they must let off a lot of steam that way. I felt like crying many times that night, but felt I shouldn't.

"The strangest, most disconnected thoughts flash through your mind when you believe you are about to die and have considerable time to think about it.

"I thought of our two children at home, who were at camp, and the fact that they would be orphans. My husband and I never flew on the same plane, for the very reason that we didn't want them to be orphans, and now look—because we had decided to come home by boat, these two children were not only going to be orphans, but were going to be minus one brother and sister as well.

"I thought of so many things I had meant to do, and cursed myself for not having done more of them. And there were so many things I wanted to do. Life had suddenly become infinitely precious and desirable (and look at me now—I am in this hospital because I wanted to destroy, deliberately, that same life that was handed back to me that night on the *Doria*).

"Strangely, I found myself wishing I had finished the story I had been reading to Bobby before dinner. He had been ordered to bed by the ship's doctor, with an infected throat and temperature of 103. Now, neither he nor I would ever know how the story ended.

"I thought, 'How inane to have gone to the hairdresser today—my hair will look great after an immersion in the ocean.' I promised God countless things if He would just get us out of this situation alive.

"Two things stand out in my memories of that night. One concerned the two priests who were passing around the last-communion cup during those hours of waiting. Call it fate, or the will of God, but as we were finishing our bridge game just before the collision, the two priests were folding up their Scrabble board, and we asked them to join us for a drink. At first they said 'No'; then they changed their minds. When we saw them on the *Ile de France*, they told us that when they had gone below to get their life jackets, their cabins were completely obliterated. The other thing was humorous. When the ship's doctor saw Bobby scurrying around the decks of the *Ile*, he pointed a finger at him and said, 'I thought I told you to stay in bed, young man.' "

"Did you panic?" my doctor asked.

"Yes, I panicked, but inside myself only. I couldn't show it, on account of the children, and I knew also that if one person 'let go,' there would be mass hysteria. The passengers really had to control themselves; as far as being any help went, the crew, by and large, might as well have been playing pinochle.

"This panic was real, and the terror of contemplating jumping off a sinking ship at night into the cold sea with two children was only too real—yet this was a panic I could control, because it had a reason, and a name. The panics I have felt during my illness have been, and are, incomprehensible, and nameless, and fill me full of inexplicable terror. I can't put a tag on them; perhaps this is why they are beyond my control."

"Are you afraid of boats now?"

"Yes. Only my love of deep-sea fishing overcomes my fear sufficiently to get me to venture on the water, but I'm certainly not happy. I have to stay in sight of land or I really do panic. If the slightest ripple appears on the water, my instinct is to run the boat up on the nearest bit of land, rocky or sandy, I don't care, and to hell with the boat. I'm not too unreasonable–provided I stay in sight of land, I will go canoeing, rowing, putt-putting, or sailing; but now and then I get the illogical feeling that I can't swim, when actually I swim like a fish. The way I feel now, I doubt if anyone could get me to cross the ocean again. Maybe I should have gotten right back on an ocean liner after the *Doria* disaster, like one gets right back on a horse, after a bad spill, but the fact is that I didn't. Shortly after the *Doria* episode my father and stepmother and one of my half-sisters were on their way from Long Island to visit us at Martha's Vineyard, when their boat ran aground on the rocks off Woods Hole, and they were almost drowned. My father, who was just recovering from an operation, had to cling to the side of the boat until the Coast Guard had carried out an extraordinary rescue. Needless to say, he was badly shaken up. I feel, all in all, that boats have let this family down. I used to think they were a pretty safe form of transportation.

"I'll have to get over the violent claustrophobia I get in planes, won't I? I won't be able to go anywhere, and I love to travel. I'll have to get over my claustrophobia, period."

"I think you are beginning to get over it."

Another day: All of a sudden I have phlebitis in my left leg. I was allowed out to lunch with a friend, and when I stood up after lunch, my leg gave way, and I fell down. I saw, with a good deal of apprehension, that my leg was a nasty shade of purple.

Now I have to be completely immobilized, with more needles stuck into me, and so much bloodletting that I'm positive I won't have any blood left. Where the hell did this come from? You're not supposed to acquire a disease in a hospital, you're supposed to get rid of the one you've got. This is the last straw, and I feel like a very ill-tempered camel.

When my doctor asked how I felt this morning, I snarled, "How do you think?"

Another day: I asked my doctor this morning, "How will I ever solve it all? I want to get well faster. You don't tell me enough about *how* to get well. I get the feeling, furthermore, that you don't want me to ask you how I am doing because I think you would rather not tell me, so everything kind of hangs in the middle of nowhere—like me."

"I can't fill you full of revelations about yourself. All this may seem a slow and stumbling way to you, but it is the only way. All I can do is to help you find the way."

Another day: My doctor says I must face the unhappy relationship between my husband and myself, and the fact that it must be terminated. This is tough to face, and it makes me feel sick to think how hard it will be on the children. After my peculiar and upsetting absence from them, this sadness must be added to their lives. This is what has torn at my heart for so long. I wish to God it could be otherwise, but I know that I have no chance of getting well, or staying well, if my husband and I continue in this marriage.

I said to my doctor today, "Never again will I let an untouching, unclose, uncommunicative relationship develop. I know now that without communication you can lose each other. When I was a child, I had a governess who used to punish me by not talking to me for days on end. This form of punishment drove me into a state of panic."

My doctor asked, "When did you first feel you were losing touch with your husband?"

"I can't remember any particular moment. We simply had a completely different way of looking at life. Gradually, and I can't tell you how or why, my husband and I reached a point where we couldn't communicate at all. The whole relationship made me feel trapped—in fact, I began to develop quite violent claustrophobia. I wouldn't let myself think of divorce, and yet, there was no way we could get through this impenetrable wall that had sprung up and grown between us. As you know, I sought psychiatric help—I was married to a man who would not seek it. Little by little, the lack of closeness, verbal and otherwise, threw me into a state of panic."

"Why do you think you got married at such a young age?" asked my doctor.

"I think I was obsessed with making a united cozy home of my own, with children of my very own, a home that would never be split, and would not have children going back and forth between parents. I wanted to get away from a divided home. Such is the optimism, unrealism, and arrogance of youth, that you think you can do better than those who went before you. Well, you learn, but the hard way. I married for the wrong motives, and I made one of the first men who cared for me into something he had to be, in my mind. In my eagerness to make a united home, I never stopped to think, 'Is this man really what you think he is, and are you suited to each other?' It takes a long time to outgrow this immature tendency and to see that no one man can fulfill all the roles you may need because you have lacked or been deprived of certain essential relationships in your life.

"Perhaps because I had missed my father so much as a child, I was afraid to let a man go out of my life, even though I knew he wasn't right for me. I didn't have the faith that he might stick around if I didn't marry him. I know one thing now, you can't run away from an unpleasant situation by getting married. How could I have been so naïve as to think you could, particularly since I had been surrounded by unhappy marriages for most of my young life?"

"I am glad you have reached this degree of self-understanding," said my doctor, "but in the process you have been tearing yourself apart, over your marriage, your children, and your sense of failure, haven't you?"

"Oh, God, yes, I have."

6

Transitional Period

Today I heard something completely wonderful—the sound of my own laughter. I can talk and joke and enjoy myself some of the time, without withdrawing into my shell like a timid tortoise.

I can talk on the telephone, too, and I want to reach out to other people now. I told my doctor, "I can read, and the words don't blur. I don't identify with everyone and everything bad and awful anymore. The words mean what they are supposed to mean, and the people are just themselves, not me. I can enjoy my television set, too, and listen to the radio. I can absorb what I see and hear. I think about what it really means, and I have ideas about it. You can't know how it feels to have had your mind die and to have it come alive again. My memory is back, and I can look ahead. Do you know how wonderful that is? There was no future for so long, only a past that I could not bear to think about, and an unbearable, agonizing, torturing present."

"Can you remember as well as you used to before you became ill?"

"I think so. I just can't remember anything about a lump of time before and during the shock treatments. Will I ever remember that time?"

"Probably never."

"So be it; but I feel I am in control of my mind again." And yet it's frightening to have lost, forever, a part of your life.

Another day: My doctor came in today to discuss some medicine he is going to give me, and the possibility of going home for a short visit.

He asked, "Are you afraid to go home, or do you want to?"

"Both," I answered.

"You tell me when you feel ready. I don't want to push you."

"I love you."

"Why?"

"Because you made me well."

"Well, now, just a minute. I *helped* to make you well, but in the long run you did a lot to make yourself well."

"Never, you did it all, and I love you. You gave me keys to all kinds of new doors that I knew were there all along, but I couldn't find the keys to unlock them. And I remember the feeling I had in the closed place that I had no key to the prison of my mind. Now I feel as if I were beginning to have a key."

"Well, I can see how you might be enthusiastic now, but everything will fall into perspective eventually. Don't forget, there were a lot of moments when you resented me and–"

"I never resented you. Naturally, no one likes to have to strip his soul to the bone in front of someone else, or suddenly have shock treatments, but you were right, don't you see? And don't tell me I have a father complex because I am dependent on you, and that I have no marriage to go home to. I know all this."

"Well, you are going to need me for a while, just for a while."

"I know that. I will need you backing me up for a good long time, but dependent or not dependent, don't spoil it all. I have reached a peak on the way up, and I have something to celebrate."

"I know, but you won't stay on that peak. There will be valleys between this peak and the next."

"I know that."

"You will get independent when the time comes; don't worry. I don't know when, but the time will come."

"Well, the time hasn't come now, and I get the whole realistic, practical message. I am not manic–just happy. It has been such a long time since I was happy. Please join me on my magic carpet for now."

He smiled.

Another day: I was allowed to leave the hospital and to go out to lunch and to the movies with a friend. We had a happy lunch, and I felt elated with my freedom. We went to see *The Nun's Story.* I was enjoying it thoroughly until a scene which takes place in an insane asylum. I watched the patients staring vacantly, simpering, and muttering, and I began to shake, and turned icy cold, and I fainted. I regained consciousness in an ambulance on the way back to the hospital. I had never fainted in my life before. I was haunted by the movie. How strange that we should have picked that particular movie. I loved the book, which I read two or three years ago, but I had not remembered the part about the insane asylum at all.

I asked my doctor, "Shall I ever stop identifying with insane people, even now, when I am so much better?"

"Yes, you will, over a period of time."

"How much time?"

"I can't answer that with any degree of certainty."

Another day: With a sense of dread and fear, and yet longing, I went home for a short visit. I felt I was looked upon with suspicion, curiosity, and even some hostility. I felt also that I was being judged and weighed and found wanting. It wasn't anyone's fault. I think we were all trying too hard. I was self-conscious, so that I did and said everything wrong. I performed badly, and I was a miserable flop.

Nothing looked familiar, not my cherished flowers, shells, photographs—nothing. I felt the children were strangers to me, and this feeling upset me to such an extent that I became irritated because I felt their table manners had slipped while I'd been away. But I knew that above all I must say nothing until we regain our former relationship. But how can we? I don't know how or where to start. I felt completely disoriented. Like the muscles of one's body, when they have been weakened by disuse from a physical illness, my mind was trying to make its first tentative steps away from the totally alien world of the hospital, and it failed badly.

I felt unwanted and unloved, and in spite of every effort not to, I broke down and wept in front of my son, who was home from school for the weekend. I told him that he and the other children were better off without me, that I was "out of it all," useless, and queer, and that I was sure he and his sisters were ashamed of me. Until this moment I had been unable and unwilling, out of pride, to communicate or show any of my feelings to my children. My son put his arms around me and said, "But, Mum, it isn't that way at all. We do love you very much, and want you home, badly." The chasm lessened a little; I felt love and tenderness and acceptance for the first time since I had come home. But the feeling did not last. I shall have to work hard to regain my children's confidence, trust, respect, and love.

I crawled back to the hospital as if to a cocoon.

"Never mind," my doctor said; "next time it will be better."

Another day: I told my doctor, "My husband said that I drove back to the hospital recklessly—in a way that was suicidal. Did I really do this, I wonder? It seems to me I always drive this way. It is the first time in almost a year, you know, that I have had the courage to drive a car, and I think I was drunk with my freedom."

"Do you still want to kill yourself?"

"No, I want to live, in the worst way. I have such a horror, though, of slipping all the way down again. I think if I did, I would never make it back up again. Please don't let me slip back, will you?"

"I will try to prevent it, and so will you."

"I am so near the shore now, I have one foot on solid land, and one not quite there yet. I need one big push to get me on it for keeps."

"I don't think it will work quite that way. You will get on really solid land over a period of time."

"Will I ever really make it?" I asked myself.

I try to telephone home more often, and I write to the children constantly. I am more natural and spontaneous now, and I have the feeling that they are beginning to think that I am a human being again.

Now I think I can face another visit home, after all. I have to be ready for my daughter's wedding, for which I shall have to try to be pretty, gay, and normal. It looms enormous, a huge obstacle to surmount.

Another day: I went home again today, and everything was a little better. I felt more at ease with the children, and I believe they felt more at home–like their old selves–with me.

I went out to lunch with a good friend with whom I always feel relaxed. I wore a yellow linen dress, and she said she had never seen me look so pretty. I hummed, "I feel pretty, oh so pretty," all the way home in the car. I want to look pretty. What a wonderful feeling to care again! It is an exhilarating feeling to be able to drive the car without feeling trapped in it, or that I have to get out of it every other mile, like I used to.

This morning I woke up full of dread. It smothered me. "Why," I thought; "why?" Is this the great so-called light after the darkness? In addition, I felt completely disoriented. I can't make it, I can't. "Try," I said; "try." I studied everything in my room, and the view out of my window, trying to feel that I belonged here. "I am me," I thought, "except that I can't remember exactly how to be the person I was before I became sick. Maybe it is just as well. Nevertheless, I would like to remember. I must know, in case I start losing myself again. Until I am quite sure who I am, or have had a chance to make a new me, I must know what I used to be like."

I made a few suggestions about my daughter's wedding, but everything was well taken care of. I felt hurt, left out, and not needed. I know no one meant to hurt me. I know my daughter must be very disappointed and sad inside that I was not there in the beginning to help her plan her wedding. It would have been such fun to do it together.

I'll have to start thinking about what I should wear to the wedding. What on earth does a bride's mother wear? I can't face surmounting this enormous problem.

One of the men who works on our place announced that the roses have some kind of blight. I am sure he would have been happier if he could have told me that a plague of locusts had stripped every leaf off every tree, bush, and flower, just in time for the wedding. I really don't care; there is nothing I can do about it anyway. I feel that I should be able to cope better with this type of problem, but I can't just now; therefore, it makes me impatient to even hear about it, and then I get annoyed at myself. I guess I really do care. It is my feelings of inadequacy that bother me most of all.

"It was a little better, though, wasn't it?" asked my doctor.

"Yes, a little, but I feel as if I were hanging outside the window of a tall building and my hands are too tired to go on gripping, and I'm going to have to let go and fall."

"It will get better and better, some ups, some downs, but the ups will seem higher and the downs will seem less low."

Another day: When are you ready to leave this type of hospital? When? Here I found affection, caring, and trusting. Will I find this "outside" too? How am I going to bridge the gap, the enormous chasm, between this hospital and home? This has been my world for so long–such a circumscribed, safe world. Shall I have the courage to leave it?

My doctor and I know that the time has come for me to leave. This not altogether unpleasant, somewhat childish state of irresponsibility and passivity cannot continue–I must start trying to make decisions on my own, for what is freedom except the capacity to make decisions? Somewhere I lost this capacity, and thereby forfeited my freedom. If you cannot think, how can you make decisions? I believe I have reached the point where I can, again, think.

How strange that I shall miss this room, with its

view of the George Washington Bridge, and the neat flower beds.

Another day: I asked my doctor, "Suppose the phone hadn't rung that night I was standing on the railing of the balcony of our apartment? Suppose I had not answered it, and that particular chance to commit suicide had not been interrupted? Do you think I would have done it? I am sure I wanted to be stopped."

"We'll never know, will we?"

"But how many people might have been stopped just by some lucky chance, and still be alive and well and happy again? If they had just gotten over that one last worst hump. It was a miracle for me–that phone call–wasn't it? When I think of what I might have missed, a chance to pick up the pieces (oh, I know I have a long way to go yet) and to start living, I am aghast!"

"I am glad you feel that way."

"You know, I feel guilty and humble at the same time about this illness. I think it made me suffer more than anything else I have ever known. But when I read, for example, about what happened to the Jews in concentration camps during the war, the horror and the suffering of it beyond believing, and I realize that *that* was real, I am overwhelmed with guilt. Yet, you know, the things that a sick mind can conjure up and believe to be real are a terrible form of suffering and horror too. The only difference is that this suffering goes away–at least it has in my case."

"There is no doubt that the anguish a sick mind can produce is indescribable. Even I, who know so much about it, can only understand and feel through listening, because I am lucky enough to have had a healthy mind all my life. And, remember, there was a time when you thought your suffering would never end."

"When I go, I shall be sorry for those who are still not free, but glad that I am. I shall have to face my failures, my divorce, but I am free to do it, and I can make a success or failure of my life from here on in. My blinders are off, and I think I shall have a better perspective of what is important and what is not, and I shall keep the unimportant out of the important part of my life. I think I shall be a better person. I know myself better, and perhaps someday I can become the person I always wanted to be. I know my faults, but I accept them now. I feel the pain of the realization that I can never be perfect, and I accept this. I hope I shall not be as afraid as I have been. I know there will be less need for my protective shell. I shall never deceive myself again.

"Above all, I shall not forget how I felt during this illness, and when I am really well and strong again, I shall help those who, like me, need help."

On my first trip back to Psychiatric Institute to see my doctor, I gave a taxi driver the address of the Institute. He said, "Why are you going there; that's a place for nuts, isn't it?"

Without thinking, I said, "Oh, I work there."

How could I be such a traitor to my alma mater, when the place has been my world for so long, and I owe it so much? I must start *now*, ridding myself of any shame I may feel, and strengthening my courage to enable me to say with some degree of dignity, "I was a *patient* at Psychiatric Institute."

How do you tell people that you are still the same person? Do you say that nothing happened to you, when something almost beyond description did? That dark corners in your mind have been illuminated, so that you are different in some ways, and yet the same?

People in general will not see a great change in me, and the world has not changed in my absence—in fact, most people are unaware of how long I have been gone, or how far away. But inside, I feel some change, not to be seen by the rest of the world. I have attained a better perspective on my life. Perhaps your mind must be broken and put back together again so that you can see just how many gifts God gave you and how to use them. I will have to fight hard to hold on to this image.

As my doctor once said, the effect of my illness on the children has not been permanent. As soon as I was all right, so were they. Perhaps they were even better, because they were more generous, more tolerant, more understanding, and they gained in courage and closeness to each other during a tough time of confusion and adjustment. Now they ask why my husband and I waited so long to get a divorce. I answer, "Partly for your sake—we tried to hold the home together for you." They say that they are grateful for the sacrifice but that it wasn't worth it. I don't want them to think of it as a sacrifice. And now that they are older, I believe they can understand why the effort failed. I pray that someday I can make up to them for the loss of the atmosphere of married love, of which they were deprived.

Since mind and body are closely related, there is a pattern which repeats itself, a cycle. You get physically sick, and some of the mental-illness symptoms come back. Even though all the other stresses and bad circumstances no longer exist, the shame and guilt of being physically sick again, and the feeling of being abandoned in a hospital, are still there, and so is the dread of being out of things and losing the mainstream again.

I had to have an operation at a New York medical center where I could not get a room in the private pavilion, so I was put in the neurological wing. A resident, who had my old records, gave me a rough time. He questioned me about my mental illness, my depression, my thoughts of suicide, all of which was very upsetting to someone already sensitive about such topics. I know that the questions would not have been asked if I had been in any other part of the hospital where there was no record of my having been a patient in the neurological part. The questions this resident asked caused resentment and loss of faith in myself again and generated old doubts and fears. I said nothing at the time to him, but I hated myself for being so passive, and decided to have it out with him. I felt a lot better after I had talked to him. I told him, "Please try never to be unaware about a former mental patient's feelings. He is already so troubled about physical and mental stability and emotional health that the attitude with which he is approached can cause grave doubts in his mind about himself, withdrawal, and a relapse." I don't think he understood what I meant, but I do know he made it harder for me to reach out to people, to feel normal, and in touch with those I love.

I had a very bad experience today. I went to sit with a judge, who is a friend of mine, at Children's Court. The problems of disturbed children have always interested me. After I left my friend, I have no idea where I went. That night, late, one of my children found me cowering in the corner of the living room of our apartment, in the dark. There were eight hours of my time unaccounted for, and I was terrified that I was losing my mind again. I must have seen and heard things at the court that frightened me, and maybe I wanted to forget. I am still not all that strong yet.

I want to work at a place where people who have just been discharged from mental hospitals come to, before they can resume their former lives again. But it is too difficult for me now. I identify too much with the very people I want to help. I must reach a point where I can say, "I felt that way too," but now I can only say, "I feel that way too."

The fear of the fear of thinking of suicide still comes unbidden, and yet I know that life is the most precious gift of all. I can rid myself of the fear most of the time. You have to have almost destroyed your life to realize just how precious it is—every second; not a moment can be wasted. Most mornings I am as excited as a child. There is so much to look forward to each day. Some mornings I still wake up with an inexplicable dread, but on the whole these mornings are fewer. I am aware of a rebirth in me that is better than being born. I really appreciate birth this time. I must learn to savor the moment, and concentrate on it only. I must not look behind with regret or ahead with doubts and fears the way I used to.

The fear of losing me, or my identity, again is still with me. The fear of "going back" remains the worst of all. I say to myself, even if I did have to "go back," and I don't think I will, I made it once, and I can make it again, and it will be easier next time because I know more about the kind of treatment I need. I don't always believe I could make it again, though.

I have a friend who is in a mental hospital. She cannot answer the phone, and I hear from her doctor that she is "doing as well as expected," words only too familiar to me. I want to go to see her, but I am having a hard time screwing up my courage to do so. I must get over this fear that if I go back to a mental hospital to visit someone that I will be kept there.

I continue to need a helping hand. There are patterns and reflexes triggered off by physical illness sometimes, sometimes not, which I cannot handle alone. Right now, I must not allow the fears to pile up again. The time will come, unforced and unbidden, when I shall need no help. I shall learn to take over the controls should my pilot fail. I must have faith that these fears will pass and that they will not be with me forever. I must, above all, believe that it need never be the end, as I once thought it had to be, if I ever get sick again.

If I find myself slipping too badly, I get help right away. When I can't read, or play the piano, or I start to withdraw, I try to work on manual things. I see my doctor and talk things out with him. I may get some medicine. I make myself do things and see people in order not to become isolated again. Yet I must avoid too much pressure at these moments. Therefore I am careful not to get overcommitted, because not being able to live up to my commitments brings me a feeling of failure. I must be careful not to push myself beyond my physical strength, in my eagerness to make up for all the lost time, because I happen to feel extra strong at the moment. I must remember I will have my weak moments too. I am no longer ashamed of taking a drug to help me, any more than a diabetic is ashamed of taking his insulin.

I must not become discouraged because I still have to struggle to hold my body and my mind together. I must learn to recognize that my sources of energy are limited, and that is one of the reasons I feel there is so little time. I must try to be less intense about everything I do, because the pressure of no time and intensity drain the energy I have.

Roosevelt was right when he said, "You have nothing to fear but fear itself." If I do not fear that I will have the fear of committing suicide, I will rid myself of the obsession. As one of my children said, "Why would anyone want to kill himself?" How could I have tried to throw my life away? Your life is not just yours–it belongs to so many people.

I have remarried. This time the motives were right.

My husband was told he must be my strength for a while. He sees me when I begin to lose myself, my personality. The doctor told him I have great strength and some courage, otherwise I would have taken my life long ago. It was only by using tremendous will power that I clung to my almost vanished identity, because I remembered just enough to know that my future might hold some potential for good. He was told that if he could help me over occasional brief humps and stand by through continued psychiatric help that our future would hold great hope. How brave of my husband to take me on. He believes I have a wonderful doctor, so he can't help but put his faith in him as I do, and trust in him as I have for so long, and believe with me that our life together will work out, and that I have a chance to stay well. He has made me feel valuable and loved and has helped me to be strong enough to stand on my own two feet and to feel that I am worth something. I no longer feel lost and without meaning, and I feel like sharing my happiness with others, by trying to give them some of my joy. How gentle and understanding and sensitive he is about my problems and fears—because always in a corner of my mind, lurks the fear, "Shall I slip back into the abyss?" When these fears become terrors, I want to go back and hide in the hospital, because it seems safe. We will lick these feelings.

Of course I have worried about my children as regards their heredity and their environment. Have they inherited any tendencies or predispositions toward mental illness? I have been reassured on this point by several expert doctors. First of all, there is other blood in their veins than mine; in the second place, they have had a cozy, intimate, loving environment, in spite of divorce; in the third place, doctors know so much more today than they ever did about how to avert mental illness. I watch my children extremely closely, with a very aware eye for any symptoms of disturbance, and am very quick to seek professional help before anything can build up into a major problem. How I wish I had had help during certain periods of my life. My children have been, on the whole, very healthy physically. Thank God their record of poor physical health has not approached mine. It is recognized that children and adults are constituted of two units, physical and psychological. The psychological unit can upset the stability in the physical unit, and vice versa. In no sense have any of my children had a really poor health record, except for my son when he was very small, and he has outgrown it.

I must accept the fact that my illness may recur, that I may be like a frog that succeeds in going up a wall three feet and slides back two, but he has still gained a foot. I must accept the fact that fear does and will jump out at me at the most unexpected moments, and haunt me for no apparent reason. It will continue to sweep over me in waves, but now the waves toss me back on the beach, battered, but well enough to pick myself up, and to reach solid land.

I have put tags on some of my dreads and even understand why I have them, but tags can get mislaid, and at times the dreads return, incomprehensibly and out of the blue. I must not allow them to encroach upon my new-found courage, hopes for the future, and happiness. How much longer will I have to fight so hard—forever?

My husband had to go to the hospital to have an operation, and I felt completely abandoned. Although my children were with me, I could not decide whether or not to tell them how I felt. I wanted to say, "I am scared; don't leave me now," but pride and fear of frightening them prevented me from telling them; yet children can rise to occasions of this kind. The question is, should you demand it of them?

You forget how nice other people can be. I have always been afraid to tell them my fears, and now that I do sometimes tell them, I am surprised how much it helps.

I must stop agonizing about the reasons why I was forced to get help, when someone else might not have been, in a storm perhaps far worse than mine. I must simply accept it. I was pushed or dragged over the line, and that is that.

I must accept the sudden occasional desire that I have to run away from a situation in which I feel trapped. It happens less frequently now, and the violent claustrophobia I had is diminishing gradually. I can put it in perspective, and regain my sense of proportion, and make myself see that I am not really trapped.

Out on a ranch in Wyoming one rainy day, I joined a group of children in one of the barns to learn how to tool a leather belt. All at once my remembrance of occupational therapy at the sanitarium I had hated so much swept through me. I rushed to open the barn door to get out, and stood in the rain, breathing the air, looking at the mountains, and feeling my freedom. I was panicky, but I made myself go back in the barn. I told myself, "I don't have to do this; I am doing it because I want to. The feelings of suffocation and claustrophobia will pass."

I must realize that I am no longer trapped, that so

many situations can be changed, and I don't have to accept them passively and forever, or think so little of myself as to endure them indefinitely. Nothing is completely rigid. I must have the courage to change what I can. I must not get so emotionally upset that I cannot see the alternatives. Where there are alternatives, there is no need to feel trapped.

My nightmares are still bad, but now I can stop them from intruding into my waking hours.

What was a friend when I was sick? A friend was someone who stayed with me when I needed him or her, who tried to understand, and above all feel with me, no matter how hard it was. No matter how insurpassable the chasm between us, he or she kept trying to pierce through that terrible wall of isolation. Just after I had recovered from the acute phase of my illness, a friend was a person who made me feel at ease–who asked no questions but was ready and anxious to listen should I want to talk.

What do people mean when they say, "She's not the type to have a mental illness!" Who knows who is the type? Who really knows what goes on inside of his fellow humans? How can people say, "But you were always so balanced, so normal." What is balanced? What is normal? We can all put on an act up to a point, but who is to determine exactly the bounds of normality? Many people have been and are eccentric, different, but harmless to themselves and to others, and some of them have been and are geniuses.

My doctor, said, "Think of your illness as an emotional disturbance, not a mental illness, because it is more comforting to know that it doesn't damage your mind." I wish I had been shown this difference in terms sooner.

I do not think that one must reject one's past completely, no matter if it consisted of some failures. If you do reject it, you draw nothing from it. You cannot redeem your past, but you can use it to go forward.

I am learning that there is a rhythm, a pulse to life. There is a time to buck the current and a time not to, and there is a time to play life by ear. Security does not come all at once, even with the eye of affection and love on you.

We went to a beautiful place in Austria with the children for our Christmas holidays. For some unknown reason, I got into a complete panic at the church on Christmas Eve. I was able to lick it. I watched the peasants ski down to church carrying lighted torches. I listened to the singing of "Silent Night" in every language, and I joined in and felt part of the human race again. I wept with joy as I said to myself, "I can go anyplace in the world and be all right. I must have faith that everywhere in the world there are people like these, like me, and I no longer have to feel like an outsider."

On an island in Greece I walked past an insane asylum. I saw the patients standing along the fence, staring vacantly. They haunted me all day. Once I would not have associated with them or identified myself with them, but now I do. A woman who has lost a child, yes; you expect that, and you dread it because you know it can happen to you, and you can feel with her and for her. But this, these human beings behind bars for what looks like forever, no. Your imagination never stretched that far before, but now it does. It couldn't happen to you, but it did. I walked away saddened and depressed; the warm sun of Greece had gone behind a cloud. I think of these people all over the world as the forgotten ones. There seemed to be no light and no life in the place, and it appeared to be empty, even though it was full.

That night the clop-clop of horses pulling carriages along the Esplanade reminded me of a wooden chess set we bought in Italy, just before sailing home from Italy on the *Andrea Doria*. We had driven to the store where we bought the chess set in a horse and carriage. We had the chess set mailed to us, so we received it. Everything else we had collected on the trip was on the bottom of the ocean. Yet how lucky we were that we were all safe, but I felt fear and sadness when I heard the horses.

The next morning at the Rome airport, walking out of the terminal building, I saw a woman and two little children saying a tearful farewell to the man of the family, who was going to join them in America soon. This exact same scene was enacted on the dock in Naples before boarding the *Andrea Doria*, and I remember hoping in the lifeboat I was in that the Italian family were not among the missing, and that the father would join them in America. A flash, a constriction of my heart, a sadness, that is all.

Back on the ranch in Wyoming where first I lost my mind, I am aware of the contrast between that day and today. Today I tied up my horse and went back to a beaver dam where I had seen little pools in which I wanted to catch brook trout. Buttercups and moss grew all over the banks. I could hear my horse munching clover. The air smelled of sagebrush in the sun. My husband was downstream. All the children were happy, out on their horses. Such a flood of joy overwhelmed me that I had to sit on the bank. I prayed, "Lord, let me stay this way always; let me believe that I am really here to stay. I will work at it every minute of the day, no matter how discouraging it may be at times. Let me have enough faith in me so that I will never again get lost in a world that is neither alive nor dead."

Conclusion

During my recovery I realized how very hard mental illness is on the people closest to the patient, who unknowingly makes demands that are, at times, almost impossible to fulfill.

Yet beyond any describing, you need the love and patience and faith of those you love and who love you, for you feel you have lost their love and have little or no love for yourself or faith in yourself. You need every encouragement to reidentify with the human race because your courage has come to a very low pass and it does not quite dare to peek around the next corner. You have been gone so long, and you have been so far away.

A patient just released from a mental hospital feels, whether correctly or incorrectly, that he is being watched with some degree of doubt and suspicion and even with hostility. He is paralyzed by the fear of doing or saying anything, because it may seem strange and be misinterpreted. Whether his feelings about how others are reacting to him may be only in his mind, nevertheless he feels keenly that others are sizing him up and perhaps discussing him (and what is more, some of them really are doing just that). He is compelled continuously to prove himself in some way–to pass some kind of test and jump through hoops–in order to be readmitted to the society of "normal" people. He becomes so anxious to prove that he is normal that he often does do and say strange things that make him appear "different" and unlike himself. There is bound to be at first a strained atmosphere, and the ex-patient becomes bewildered and feels rejected and frightened.

How well I remember those first visits home–the totally abnormal and painfully strained atmosphere that prevailed, compounded of suspicion, hostility, bewilderment, and feelings of rejection on all sides. I would crawl back to the basically hated and resented hospital as if to a sanctuary of safety and refuge. How unfair it seemed that I had to leap over so many tormenting hurdles all at once.

Unfortunately there still exists a vague and intangible stigma attached to mental illness. There is an almost unadmitted shame and aura of mystery and a desire to keep it hidden–all outworn relics of the past, yet they continue today in the attitudes of many people.

Why should there be completely different reactions from people toward a broken mind than there are toward a broken limb? The mind, in many cases, has as good a chance to heal as, say, a shattered leg.

I know about the case of a young medical student who suffered a breakdown during his second year of medical school. It took months of wire-pulling, long after he had become well, to get him reinstated in any school of medicine. My feeling is that he might conceivably be more than ordinarily understanding and sympathetic toward his patients because of his own experience.

Is it fair that an ex-mental patient should drag his illness around for the rest of his life any more than any other kind of illness?

It's true that in this day and age there is far more understanding and compassion toward the mentally ill than in the past, but nevertheless the patient who has been confined to a mental hospital, as compared to any other type of hospital, is still aware of a certain degree of shame attached to his confinement. Every person who has been mentally ill is terrified of being rejected—so much so that he does not always tell the truth about himself. Until understanding reaches total acceptance, a person who has been in a mental institution will feel different and ashamed.

I feel that during my mental illness, my children—the very ones who most needed understanding of my condition—rather than being told the truth were the ones who were kept most in the dark.

This was due in part to a lack of understanding, a breakdown in communications, and to a misguided desire to protect them from the truth. Truth, in the last analysis, is far and away the easiest thing for a child to face. There is nothing more frightening than the unknown and the misunderstood. Lies, half-truths, evasions, embellishments, attempts to "tidy" it all up—all directed toward an effort to deny the actual fact—although well meaning, end by making the illness appear far worse to a child than is necessary. My children were old enough to understand a good part of the truth.

When I was over the first part of my illness, I received a letter in the hospital saying that one of my children was becoming a problem in boarding school. The child's behavior was unusual for him, his marks were slipping, and the last straw was that he returned from Easter vacation with a live duck that he kept in his room at school. My first instinct was to laugh. Obviously I was aware of the impossibility of each child in the school keeping a duck and that my child had broken a rule. But I knew that this rather pathetic action was a reaction to many other things. This child had always loved animals. I believed he was lonely, and I thought there was a good bit of defiance and bravado in his gesture. I put through a telephone call to the headmaster and tried to explain what I thought had happened to my child. I told him I thought he had been carrying a big load of worry and uncertainty about me. The headmaster said that he had no idea that anything had been wrong with me, except a mild ulcer. I told him as much of the truth as I could manage. He was terribly distressed not to have been better and more accurately informed, because he then would have been able to handle my child quite differently. He would have helped and supported him. My child was too proud, perhaps ashamed or confused, to admit he needed help. Furthermore, it was difficult for him to ask for help because he had no real knowledge of what the problem was.

This breakdown of communication among school, child, and home was extremely harmful. My child needed shoring up, not tearing down, and above all, it was distressful for him to live in uncertainty and doubt. As for me, the incident ended by upsetting me badly, because I became aware of what my illness might be doing to my children.

As far as my children were concerned, I, their mother, had disappeared into the blue, with the explanation that my ulcer had come back again. But naturally they wondered why I didn't write or telephone as I always had done in the past. They were bewildered and aware that they were not being told the truth. They knew that something was queer and that I was not to be seen.

There was no help I could give them then. I was lost to myself, and to them, and to the whole world.

When one of my children finally was allowed to come to see me, in the second hospital I was in, she wept. At first I thought it was the emotion of seeing me again, but she kept repeating, "You're not locked up. You're not tied up. There aren't any pads on the wall, and there are no bars on your windows, and this is a regular room." She had been living with a snake-pit image for God knows how many months and it had wreaked far more havoc than the truth, which was explainable and comprehensible.

How much better it would have been if she had

been provided with a clear description of the place I was in, even when it was locked, and been kept abreast of some of the treatment that was being given to me to make me well. Then she herself would have become aware of my progress.

My eldest daughter was allowed to visit me during the time I was having shock treatments. Although she knew I was having the shock treatments, no one had told her that my mind would be rambling and that I would be incoherent; consequently, she was indescribably and unnecessarily upset.

If the remaining "well" parent, or grandparent, or some relative is unable to handle a coherent explanation that a child can accept, then I think children should see the doctor taking care of their mother or father so that they are part of the problem and do not feel completely and inexplicably abandoned. God knows it is hard enough to explain mental illness to anyone and most of all to a child. An expert who is knowledgeable about all the different age levels of understanding of children can tell each one what he is capable of absorbing. This is perhaps a distinction an amateur might overlook, since he is inclined at times to treat children as a group and to forget that each is at a very different age level of understanding and is a distinct individual. I think that most doctors would not turn down such a request from his patient's relatives, because the problem is a family problem.

In the confusion everyone is too busy to worry about what a child may be suffering. And yet it is not inconceivable that a child may be faced more than once in his life with the need to understand either himself or someone else who is mentally ill. Therefore the more truth he knows, the easier it will be for him should such an occasion arise in his adult life.

However, the family should not meddle in the treatment of the patient. Above all the doctor must never appear to be in cahoots with the patient's family or the patient will lose all trust in his doctor and will no longer talk with him intimately.

There is an unfortunate misconception that only people with money can afford and indulge in the luxury of a "nervous breakdown," supposedly resting in some posh private sanitarium. Never in my life did I rest less than during my illness. A tortured mind cannot rest; it leaves no peace and no escape.

Mentally ill patients, it seems to me, one and all, are brought to their knees regardless of age, background, class, color, weakness, or strength–arriving there by very different routes; nonetheless, they are there. All are sick, some more, some less, and almost all are living in an incredible nightmare.

It is true that people with money who are mentally sick get a better break than those with less money, but in the society we live in this applies to almost every area of living. It may not be right but it is true.

Money does help to cushion the shocks of life. A mentally ill person with means has many material advantages over one with less money. He has, first of all, more choices. He can change hospitals, doctors, or even elect to stay home if he is not harmful to others or himself. Trained nurses and doctors can attend him at home. If he goes to a hospital, he will certainly be more comfortable, and his living accommodations will be more attractive and private (however, when you are really ill you do not notice your surroundings; you wouldn't know if there were rushes on the floor). Later on, when you begin to emerge from your blackout, the red carpets, pool and Ping-Pong table (provided you like games), arrangements for occupational therapy, TV sets, petunia beds in the summer, and attractive surroundings are advantageous.

But most important of all, the patient with financial security will probably get well faster in a private institution, if he is going to get well, because the ratio of doctor to patient is much more favorable than in a public institution. He will have a better chance of staying in a hospital, should he choose to, long enough to become really cured. The person with money can continue his after-care with his doctor more easily and for a longer time in order to avoid a recurrence of his illness. The more fortunate man will go back to a more comfortable home, perhaps not comfortable emotionally but certainly more comfortable materially and physically. He can go away on vacations to avoid building up unbearable pressures in the future.

For those with less money there is a great need for more "in between" places where a patient who has just been released from a mental hospital can go to catch his breath and regain the courage to pick up his life again. For him there is no letup or vacation.

The unhappy fact is that many ex-mental patients suffer a relapse during the first year. Simply because they can go safely back to their community does not mean that they are permanently cured or won't be repeaters. It is immeasurably hard for them to stay well because the world has become a foreign, threatening place, impossible to cope with. They have been locked up, too isolated, too cut off, too different, too unrealistically "safe and secure" in a circumscribed world in which they feel imprisoned and yet do not dare leave.

Meanwhile, where *do* some of them go? The hospital door is always open to them but the community is not. Let us say that a person is ready to leave the hospital but he cannot go home because the same problems still exist at home that made him ill in the first place. He has to stay on in the hospital because there is no place else for him to go.

In a few cities in the country—all too few—there are centers known as halfway houses. At the one in New York, in which I became interested after my illness, the members are all in the crucial adjustment stage, between the hospital routine and a full normal life. There a member learns that he can function, that he can be needed, and that he can relax. There is nothing to hide because other members are in the same boat. He is helped back to the real world by degrees. He works in a real world and earns money. This is unlike occupational therapy in hospitals, where he most often feels that what he produces is more or less useless. Gradually he can take on a fulltime job alone, always supported by a social worker or a trained staff member who sees that he doesn't at first get a job that is over his depth. He feels that his services are required and needed, and he is no longer completely dependent. This raises his self-esteem after all the degrading feelings he has lived through. There are other social contacts in the evening, and creative activities with other members. Some apartments are leased by this in-between place where members can live together with a supervisor, establishing real, housekeeping living.

I think if an ex-patient doesn't get this kind of help, he may easily break down again. This way he gets inner faith back. Faith comes from strength beyond his own at first, but then it becomes his, and he can move on alone. Those who have lived in the shadows and been at the bottom of the abyss can understand each other without words and help each other back to the outside world.

There does exist the mistaken idea that a mental illness is a type of self-indulgence by the self-centered and selfish who allow themselves to reach a breaking point which could be avoided. What they should do is think of others who are far worse off than they are and get their minds off themselves by engaging in more and more activities with and for others. This kind of therapy can work for a time, perhaps, in mild and borderline situations, and before a person has slipped too far over the line of rationality; and it can help after a breakdown, but it does not help a mind that has become irrational. After a mental illness most patients will do all they can to pull themselves together, and what is more, they will do anything to prevent a second one, to avoid the torture they have already lived through.

I have never met a member of the medical profession who believed that mental illness was deliberate self-indulgence. A patient can no more "pull together" a broken sick mind and expect it to knit and become whole without expert help than he can expect a broken limb to knit straight without a doctor's help.

There is no physical control with which to manage the mind that is slipping or breaking, or has slipped or broken. The controls, cure-alls, and helpful therapies are no longer helpful. In fact they no longer exist; they are gone, gone with the lost mind.

It is said that we are born, like a snowflake, each one of us with a God-given and completely unique individuality. For us humans, there is inheritance. Then comes early home surroundings, and then the first steps outside the home. The interaction of what we brought with us, with what we found, makes us what we shall be. Out of our early years come the building stones on which our later life is founded. Some foundations stand forever firm, some do not.

For all mental patients, in my opinion, locked doors leave an indelible impression and create terrible feelings of dread and loss. They take away the last shred of human dignity and self-respect because the patient feels he is like a criminal entering a prison. If he already has claustrophobia, being locked up is almost unbearable. It made me rebellious, as well as terrified.

I firmly believe that an emotionally disturbed or mentally ill patient should not be thrust into a distant and alien environment if it is humanly possible to treat him otherwise. I realize that there are some mentally ill people who must be locked up, but if it is not necessary, to be put away so finally and utterly from their family and their world is harmful. I believe that the difference between the inside and the outside must be minimized so that a patient does not have the enormous gap to bridge between the closed hospital and the outside world. We no longer have the right to put a fellow human being out of sight and out of mind due to fear and guilt, often with the uneasy feeling that a hairline separates the mentally ill from the mentally healthy. The family should be drawn in so that the doctor can get a complete picture of the patient's relationship to his whole environment: home, job, friends, interests, and the world at large. Then it is possible to find out which members of his family or those with whom he associates may have contributed to his illness. A family should be treated as a unit or the job is only half done.

There is today, fortunately, a trend toward more open hospitals or psychiatric wings that are part of general hospitals, and smaller, more personal centers that are also more open. The medical profession is beginning to try part-time hospitals for mentally disturbed people in a normal community environment, where a patient can go to work during the day and return to the hospital at night. His problems can be coped with right then and there. It is a way of bringing the community into the hospital.

There is a quiet revolution away from the large security, or custodial out-of-the-way hospital, toward small active treatment centers in the community, family oriented and almost completely open.

The sense that a patient's longing for freedom is vitally important not only to him, but to others too, is of paramount importance.

Should institutionalized hospitalization be necessary, however, the atmosphere of the hospital is all-important. The patient's mood is very much influenced by everyone around him. A broken mind senses kindness like a dog or a child, and reacts accordingly. A special word or a person who shows an interest gives courage to face the time ahead. An abrupt word, or a harsh one, can bring resentment, anger, and a desire to retaliate. Even if the patient is not the one to whom the harsh word is addressed, it fills him full of fear. Even if certain noises and sights are perhaps unavoidable, and no one is to blame for them, they are terrifying because he feels "this is me too." It is difficult for harassed, overworked doctors and nurses and other attendants to remember this, but certainly many of them try their hardest to be kind and interested. The kindness, patience, and care it takes to bring a sick mind that wants to die back to the point where it wants to live again, and wants and feels ready to walk its body out the front door of the hospital to the world outside, are infinite.

One of the most important things I learned was that a patient has certain rights he is entitled to. I was so terrified at first that I was convinced I had *no* rights, and no one thought to tell me that I had any. If I had known that I could turn to a lawyer, for instance, on the "outside," I would have been less terrified, and not had the feeling that I might be locked up for life. In the bad hospital I was forbidden to make a phone call, and my mail was returned to me if I made any complaints.

It is generally believed that the following are prime factors contributing toward mental illnesses: genetic inheritance, physiochemical make-up, early environmental influences, and pressures and tensions of the moment and recent past. There are differences in opinion as to their order of importance and the degree to which each one figures. It is not from lack of courage that a person becomes mentally ill, but from an accumulation and number of shocks, anxieties, pressures, and fears to which he has been subjected since birth.

Evidently the number and accumulation of anxieties, fears, tensions, and shocks to which I was subject through the years built up and had me licked for a period of time. I developed a mental illness.

I am sure I needed help when I was a child, the kind of psychiatric treatment available today. Perhaps then my path could have been straightened or turned in such a way as to avoid the illness I was fated to have as an adult.

Since I was destined to be mentally ill, how lucky I was this happened to me in recent times when so much could be done to make me well—so well that today I am able to write about my illness. And how fortunate I was to have had a doctor who was able to give me constant attention.

I am grateful for the opportunities given me to have found finally, after bad experiences, the place and doctor, the expert treatment and constant daily care that made me well—in a place where I could fight with "them" instead of against "them" for my return to health. I am not intimating even remotely that I went through any "snake-pit" experience. I am thankful for the privilege I had of leaving hospitals that were wrong for me because they filled me with terror and horror and stripped me of the last shred of human dignity—

places that were, I believe, too rigid, too unimaginative, and perhaps even destructive for me.

I asked my doctor, who believes strongly in psychotherapy plus shock treatments and drugs, why psychotherapy helps when the going gets tough.

He said, "Suppose you had been able to talk to a trained psychotherapist whom you could have trusted when you were young, about your family problems, your illnesses, your acute fears; don't you think you could have been liberated then, instead of going through all the heartaches you did? And with understanding you would have had less guilt, too, about all your confused feelings, and could have been straightened out much earlier in your life."

He is right, of course. After the age of forty it is harder to get effective help. The poor old dog has to work awfully hard to change long-established patterns of reaction. And when all is said and done, a mental illness and its cure remain somewhat mysterious. There are no absolutes or positive answers to how and why a person becomes sick or becomes well. There are so many intangible, elusive, unknown factors involved. The possible tentative quality of a cure must be faced—and the possible necessity for continued help.

What made me well? I believe it was a combination of drugs, shock treatments, and countless talks with an extraordinarily fine doctor in whom I had complete faith and with whom I was able to establish an exceptionally good rapport. Above all, this doctor made me feel that he cared very much whether or not I got well. When I was at my sickest and lowest, if he hadn't cared I know I wouldn't have either.

Psychiatrists cannot bring about miracles, but they can help you to fight—and fight you must, perhaps for the rest of your life. There is no new shiny you; you must make do with the person you were and are. They can reassure you when you feel yourself slipping and you panic. The drugs they can give you during these painful times can tide you over what seems to you to be a loss of connection between your intellect and your emotions—when the two appear to be drawing terrifyingly apart. When they draw together again, you need less help—fewer drugs, less psychotherapy. Maybe some wonderful day you won't need any help. This, above all, is the goal you and your doctor are striving for. There is always hope.

Am I now better equipped to withstand whatever is in store for me without breaking? I hope so; I pray so; I believe so.

It was better to have had no wings for a while than to have flown on one wing for the rest of my life. Now I can use both wings. I can hope to soar.

Epilogue

I stand tonight on the balcony of our apartment in New York City, from which, many nightmares ago, I almost jumped to the street below to destroy a life that seemed to me not worth keeping alive. I know that I was alone that night as I never will be alone again. My hand and the hand of God seemed against me. I did not know then that ahead of me lay the most endless months of my life. Now life is inestimably and infinitely precious. How lucky I have been, and how good time and people have been to me.

The stars are just beginning to show. I stand alone and proud and almost free, still in need of help now and then, but almost free.

I look at the street below and watch the tiny cars and people. I can look down now without fear. I look across the street. There are lights in some of the other apartments. In one, a figure moves behind the drawn blind. I feel that he or she is a friend, my friend, and that I belong to the family of man again. I want to shout my feelings from the rooftop. I feel the poignant happiness of once more being close to my children, my husband, my family, my friends, and my home, all the more poignant because they were all lost to me for what seemed forever.

These are intoxicating feelings, and they engulf me like a wave, overwhelming me with warmth and a sense of being cherished and cherishing.

I am filled with gratitude and hope that I shall be given the strength to stay the way I am tonight and the ability to help others who are or will be the way I was.